The Complete
Microwave
Book

Front cover
Photographer: Michael Kay, Solar Studios, Croydon
Microwave cooker: Moulinex
Home economist: Annette Yates

The Complete Microwave Book

by

Annette Yates

Typeset in 11pt Times by One And A Half Graphics, 4 Linkfield Corner, Redhill, Surrey.
Printed and bound in Great Britain by Cox & Wyman Ltd., Reading, Berkshire.

Clarion: published from behind no. 80 Brighton Road, Tadworth, Surrey, England.

Contents

About The Author

Annette Yates is a trained home economist who has been enthusiastically using, and writing about, microwaves since the first domestic models were offered for sale in the UK.

Annette was born in South Wales and grew up in the Brecon Beacons. After training as a home economist in London, she became Assistant Editor of an education magazine, where she wrote her first editorial on microwaves in 1974. After that, she became involved in schools' presentations, demonstrating the microwave as part of a range of cooking appliances. Since then, as well as preparing many features on microwave and combination cookers for consumer magazines, she has also organised microwave cookery classes – for a major microwave manufacturer and in a private capacity. At one time, she was instrumental in setting up and running a microwave consumer help-line for a major food company, which included answering telephone queries, writing several leaflets and factsheets, and producing an instructional video on microwaving.

Whatever her current project, she is usually to be found creating recipes in her own kitchen – her family and friends being her best critics. When she is not in the kitchen she enjoys styling food for photography, preparing features for consumer magazines, and writing and designing newsletters and recipe leaflets. Annette is author of several cook books and is co-editor of *MICROWAVE COOK**, a quarterly newsletter which is full of useful information, recipes and special offers.

Annette is a member of the Guild of Food Writers and of the Microwave Association. She now lives in Wallington, Surrey, with her husband and two student daughters.

*MICROWAVE COOK, Pine Trees, Church Road, Earsham, Suffolk NR35 2TJ

1
The Microwave

A microwave is invaluable – particularly when used, not as an isolated appliance, but as part of your team of cooking equipment in the kitchen. Used together with the hob, grill, kettle, toaster and conventional oven, your microwave will help you to get the best results in the shortest time. So you, your family and your friends can eat good food without you, the cook, having to spend hours in the kitchen.

WHAT ARE THE ADVANTAGES OF OWNING A MICROWAVE?

- Cooking times are much shorter. In fact, conventional cooking times can be cut by as much as 60-75%.

- Food can be thawed quickly in a microwave.

- It's economical. A microwave uses about a quarter of the power needed to run a conventional oven (a combination cooker uses a little more). Added to this, cooking times are shorter and, when you make full use of a microwave, the lower the power level used, the lower the electricity consumption.

- It's versatile. Most foods can be thawed, cooked and reheated in a microwave.

- It's convenient. Snacks and meals can be prepared as and when they are needed. A microwave copes particularly well with small quantities and single portions, and in households where individuals eat at different times, a microwave is a must.

- It's easy to use. A microwave can be plugged in anywhere there is a 13 amp socket. Controls are generally straightforward to use. Oven cleaning is minimal too.

- It saves on washing up because many foods can be cooked in their serving dishes.

- Microwaves are clean and cool and can be particularly suitable for use by elderly and disabled people and by children.

- Low-fat and fat-free cooking is easy with a microwave.

- Flavour and nutritive value are excellent in foods cooked in a microwave. Many foods can be cooked simply in their own juices; others with just a little additional liquid. Also, cooking foods for the briefest time, and in the least liquid, is known to be one of the best ways to retain maximum food value. In other words, microwaving is a healthy way to cook.

IS THERE ANYTHING A MICROWAVE CAN'T DO?

- Browning and crisping are not possible unless your microwave has a grill or it is a combination cooker (see page 20).

- Frying, either in shallow or deep fat, is not possible.

- It won't successfully cook eggs in their shells.

- A microwave cannot make toast, unless it incorporates a very efficient grill.

- It cannot make pancakes though it will reheat them.

- A microwave cannot cook crusty pastry and bread, foods in batter, Yorkshire pudding, roast potatoes or soufflés, unless it is a combination cooker (see page 20).

- It is usually more economical to heat more than 300ml ($^1/_2$pt) water in an electric kettle than in a microwave.

- Even a microwave cannot speed up the cooking of some foods. Rice, pasta and pulses, for example, generally take as long to cook in the microwave as they do conventionally.

WHAT ARE MICROWAVES AND HOW DO THEY COOK FOOD?

Cooking with microwaves is quite different from conventional methods which use electricity, gas or solid fuel. In a conventional oven the walls and the air inside them are heated first. As the oven heats up, so does the surface of the food. This surface heat, in turn, is slowly conducted to the centre of the food.

In a microwave the walls and air are not heated. The microwaves pass straight into the food, to heat it directly.

Microwaves are electromagnetic waves, similar to radio and television waves. Electric energy is converted into microwaves by a valve called a magnetron. The microwaves are channelled along a wave guide, then a stirrer or paddle distributes them evenly into the cavity. Once they are inside the cavity, three things can happen to the microwaves.

1. They are *reflected* off the metal walls and bounce around inside the cavity (Fig. 1).

2. They are *transmitted* by glass, china, pottery, microwave plastics and paper (Fig. 2). So the microwaves pass straight through dishes made of these materials.

3. They are *absorbed* by the water (in particular) in food (Fig. 3). When the water molecules absorb microwave energy they become agitated and vibrate at an incredible speed – 2,450,000,000 times per second! It is this excitement which generates the heat which, in turn, cooks the food in a very short time. Microwaves can only penetrate food up to 4cm (1¹/₂ in), so anything thicker than 8cm (3 in) relies on heat from the outer areas being conducted to the centre – just like conventional cooking.

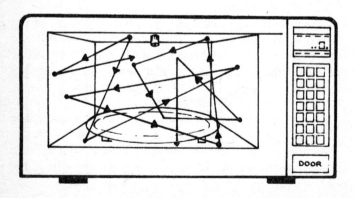

Fig. 1. The metal walls of the cavity reflect the microwaves.
(The cooker is empty for the purposes of this diagram, but remember, a microwave should never be switched on without food or drink in it.)

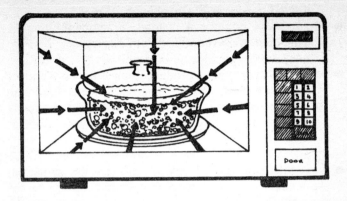

Fig. 2. Certain cooking containers allow the microwaves to pass straight through them.

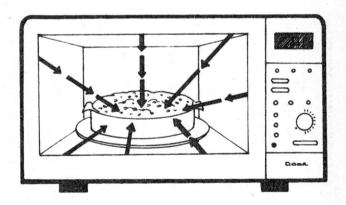

Fig. 3. Food absorbs microwaves and heats up.

ARE MICROWAVES SAFE?

- Microwaves produce a change in temperature only. They should not be confused with X-rays.

- Microwaves cannot be produced unless the cooker door is securely closed. The doors and hinges are fitted with locks, seals and cut-out switches which automatically switch off the microwaves the instant the door is opened.

- The mesh in the door lets you see inside the cavity, but the holes in this mesh are not large enough to allow the microwaves to escape. They simply bounce off the mesh back into the cooker cavity.

- British safety standards regarding leakage of microwave cookers are, as you can imagine, extremely strict. Microwaves are built to precise specifications and they are thoroughly tested before leaving the factory. When buying a microwave, look for the BEAB (British Electrotechnical Approvals Board) label for household appliances, which means that it has met safety requirements dictated by the relevant British Standard Specification for electrical safety and microwave leakage limits.

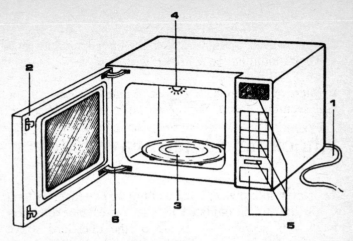

Fig. 4. The main parts of a microwave cooker.

1. Lead from oven to 13 amp plug.

2. Door fastening. There may be two or more locking devices to ensure that microwaves automatically switch off as soon as the door is opened.

3. Removable shelf or turntable. This raises the food off the floor of the cooker, so that microwaves can be absorbed from underneath too. It makes the job of mopping up spilled food easier and it also ensures that the food is in the best position to receive the microwaves (with a turntable, the food is carried around the cooker to ensure even absorption of microwaves).

4. Interior light. This usually lights as soon as the cooker is switched on.

5. Controls. Basic controls include an on/off button, a timer control and a control to adjust the microwave power level.

6. Door stop.

2
Choosing a Microwave Cooker

Choosing a microwave is an exciting experience, so long as you are not intimidated by the vast choice on offer today. This section lists some of the questions worth answering before buying. It then goes on to outline many of the features on offer today. Whether you are buying your first microwave or you are updating your current model, I hope to help you choose one which will fit in with the way you cook and eat.

How much do you want to spend?
Though price may dictate your choice initially, deciding which features you would like on a microwave will also help to narrow down a price band.

How much space do you have and where?
Will the microwave sit on the kitchen work surface or on a shelf or brackets, or will you want it built into the kitchen? Do you wish to move it around, perhaps on self-catering holidays? Remember it needs to be close to a 13 amp socket. Most models will need ventilation, so check you will be able to leave a space all round yours. Remember to position the microwave so that you have a small area of work surface next to it – for taking dishes out of the microwave and setting them down.

How do you plan to use your microwave?
If you are sure that your microwaving will be restricted to thawing and reheating, a basic model will be sufficient

with cooking, heating and defrost settings. If, however, you will want to make full use of a microwave and cook all the things it does well – soups, snacks, sauces, fish, vegetables, poultry, casseroles, fruit and puddings – you will need a model with at least 600 watts (600W) and several power levels (see page 18).

How many do you cook for?
Check the inside of the microwave. Is it big enough to take your largest casserole dish, or the largest item you are likely to cook? Will your dishes fit, and turn round, on the turntable? Even if you cook for one or two people most of the time, are you likely to cook for large numbers in the future and need a family-size microwave?

Do you already have an efficient grill?
If not, you may consider buying a microwave cooker with a grill (see page 20).

Do you regularly cook roast meals, pastry, cakes or oven-cooked food coated in breadcrumbs or batter?
If so, you may consider buying a combination cooker (see page 20) which combines the heat of a traditional oven with the speed of microwave cooking.

Will you need a good instruction/cook book?
When making your final choice, it is worth asking to see the instruction books and cook books which accompany the ovens. Some are better than others.

FEATURES ON MICROWAVE AND COMBINATION COOKERS

Controls can be mechanical or touch-control. Both are easy to use, but for accurate timing in seconds (for softening butter, for instance) choose a digital display. Touch-control panels are easy to wipe clean.

Cooker interiors can be stainless steel or plastic-coated. Both are easy to clean, and personal preference will dictate which you choose. Some models have grills which can be moved for easy cleaning behind them. Combination cookers (see page 20) often have at least one self-clean lining; some top-of-the-range models have a pyrolytic cleaning function – the oven can be heated to a temperature which is high enough to burn off any food residue.

A *turntable* helps food to cook evenly by raising it off the cavity floor so the microwaves can reach underneath, and by turning the food as it cooks. When buying a microwave with a turntable, check that your cooking containers are not so large that they prevent the turntable turning.

Wave stirrers or paddles also encourage even cooking by distributing the microwaves evenly into the cavity. Some models have both a turntable and wave stirrers.

Power output indicates the amount of microwave energy used to cook food. It currently ranges from 500W to 1000W. The higher the wattage (W) the faster the microwave cooks. Recipes in magazines and books (including this one), and cooking times on many pre-packed foods, are often based on 600-700W

If you buy a more powerful microwave (800-1000W) you will need to reduce the cooking times slightly (by about one quarter). A simpler solution is to cook on a power level (see below) which is equivalent to 600-700W (MEDIUM-HIGH/75% for example) and cook for the normal time. If you buy a less powerful microwave (500W) you will need to lengthen the cooking times by about one third.

Power levels control the amount of microwave energy entering the cavity, so food can be cooked as quickly or as slowly as you like. Manufacturers vary in the way they describe power levels – some have up to nine settings but the most useful are HIGH (100%), MEDIUM-HIGH (75%),

MEDIUM (50%), MEDIUM-LOW (30%), and LOW (10%).

A *shelf* allows more food to be cooked at the same time, though cooking times will be longer. This is because the same amount of microwave energy goes into the cavity, no matter how much food it holds, and this energy has to be shared out.

An *auto-minute* button is handy. Just press it to cook for 1 minute on HIGH (100%)

Quick/Rapid/Jet start or *Boost* is designed for quick heating of liquids and drinks in particular. It usually works on a higher power than that used for everyday cooking.

A *minute timer* or alarm can sometimes be used as an automatic timer, with no cooking involved.

Auto-defrost is a useful feature, though most foods can be thawed on DEFROST or MEDIUM-LOW (30%). Auto-defrost is controlled either by time or by the weight of the food. Some models have a sensor which weighs the food and automatically calculates the thawing time.

Auto cook/heat allows you to program in the type of food and its weight, then the oven does the rest – calculating the appropriate cooking time, power levels and, in combination cookers, the temperature. Some models have an automatic sensing device which does this. This auto-cook/heat feature is particularly useful for large pieces of meat and for ready meals.

Hold-warm puts the microwave on a lower power level to keep food warm for 15 minutes or more.

Multi-sequence cooking allows you to program the microwave to cook on a series of cooking times and power levels – for example, cooking on HIGH (100%) for a set time, switching to MEDIUM (50%) for a set time, then holding on LOW (10%) for a time.

Auto-repeat recalls the last program used.

A *memory* function stores programs – useful only if you cook the same dishes frequently.

Delay-start/Pre-set/Auto-start delays cooking for several hours if necessary, perhaps while you are out of the house. This feature is more useful in a combination cooker (for conventional or combination cooking) than in a microwave where cooking times are very short anyway and food may need turning or stirring.

A *grill* is handy for improving the appearance of microwaved food, particularly if you do not already have an efficient conventional grill. Don't expect a grill in a microwave cooker to be as powerful as a conventional grill though. It is likely to be quite small and operate only with the door closed. Some models allow simultaneous grilling and microwaving to save time. Grills with radiant elements are similar to conventional electric grills. Halogen grills give instant heat, though they are usually restricted to only one area of the cavity ceiling. A quartz grill is quick and efficient.

A *combination cooker* combines the speed of microwaving with the traditional heat of a conventional oven. Foods can be browned and crisped as well as cooked in a fraction of the usual time. A combination cooker is particularly useful if you regularly cook whole poultry and meat joints, pastry, cakes, Yorkshire pudding, soufflés and other foods which need a crisp and brown finish.

As the name suggests, a combination cooker can be used in three ways: on microwave only, on convection only (using traditional heat in °C), or with a combination of the two (often called "combination", "dual-cook" or "Hi-speed"). It is when cooking on "combination" that models vary in the way they work. There are two main types:

● where both the temperature and the microwave power level can be controlled by you;

● where there are a series of pre-set programs in which specific temperatures are already matched up with selected microwave power levels.

Your choice will depend on whether you are a keen cook who likes to experiment, and who prefers to be able to adjust temperature and microwave power in order to achieve the results you want; or whether you prefer to have it all selected for you, ready simply to press a button.

Rotisserie units feature in some combination cookers, for cooking meat and poultry on a spit, using a combination of microwaving, grilling and convected heat.

MICROWAVE LABELS

A voluntary labelling scheme for microwave cookers and food packs was introduced in 1992. It was developed by the Ministry of Agriculture, Fisheries and Food (MAFF) in partnership with microwave manufacturers, food manufacturers, retailers and consumer organisations. It is designed to help us to microwave more successfully, particularly when heating small quantities, such as ready meals for one or two. New microwave cookers are now labelled with:

● the power output based on an internationally agreed standard (IEC 705);

● a heating category letter, from A to E, to indicate the microwave's ability to heat small food packs.

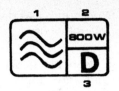

Fig. 5. The microwave labelling scheme.
1.   Microwave symbol.
2.   Power output (watts).
3.   Heating category for small packs.

All small (up to 500g) food packs which are suitable for microwaving are marked with the microwave symbol plus appropriate heating category letters and cooking times. Then, you simply match up the information on the food pack with that on your microwave cooker.

If you bought your microwave before the labelling scheme started, and you would like to know its power output under the new scheme, a free booklet, 'The New Microwave Labels', is available. It lists models together with their power output and, where possible, their heating categories. For your copy, write to Food Sense, London SE99 7TT.

3

Containers to Use

The containers which are suitable for microwave cooking are those which allow microwaves to pass straight through them and into the food. You'll probably find that many of the dishes you already own will be fit for use in the microwave. Those which have their own lids are generally the most convenient.

What to use

Ovenglass, glass ceramic, china and some pottery are suitable. Although they let microwaves pass through them, you will probably still need to use oven gloves to lift them from the microwave oven, because the heat conducted from the food makes the dishes hot. Also, because they absorb a lot of heat from the food, cooking in these containers may take slightly longer than in dishes which are specially designed for the microwave.

A wide range of microwave cookware is available today, not only in heat-resistant plastic, but also in ovenglass and ceramic glass. The most versatile are suitable for microwave, conventional oven, freezer and dishwasher – they are usually fit for cooking foods which reach a very high temperature, such as those containing a high proportion of fat or sugar. Always check the labels before buying.

Paper, soft plastics and basketware should be used only for brief heating.

What not to use

Metal containers don't allow microwaves to pass through them and, in general, should not be used for microwaving.

Some microwave manufacturers suggest using small pieces of foil to shield food and prevent it overcooking – follow their instructions carefully. Others suggest cooking some foods in foil trays – do check with the instruction book and follow the method carefully. If the manufacturer of your microwave does not advise it, don't do it – if anything were to go wrong your guarantee would be affected.

Do not use plates or dishes which are decorated with gold, silver or other metal paint. The microwaves will cause the metal to spark and blacken.

Avoid using unglazed or partly-glazed pottery, fine glass (it contains minute particles of metal), polystyrene, dairy product containers, recycled paper products and dishes which have been repaired with glue.

To test if a container is suitable for the microwave

Put the container in the microwave and place a cup containing 150ml ('/4 pt) cold water inside it. Cook on HIGH (100%) for 1-2 minutes. The outer container should remain cool while the water in the cup heats up. If the container becomes warm, this means that it has absorbed some of the microwaves – so it's not advisable to use it.

The shape matters

Circular containers are best because the microwaves reach the food equally from all sides. Though the centre usually cooks more slowly than the edges, stirring food during cooking encourages even results.

A *ring* shape produces best results and is particularly useful for foods which cannot be stirred – like cakes. There is no slow-cooking centre, so the food cooks evenly.

Straight vertical sides on a container help the food to cook evenly. Sloping sides allow microwaves to concentrate in, and overcook, food at the outer edge.

Squares and *rectangles* tend to overcook at their

corners, where the microwaves are concentrated. They often have an area in the centre which cooks only slowly.

Food wraps
Microwave bags and *roasting bags* are useful for microwave cooking. Follow the packet instructions for use. Ordinary polythene food bags are not suitable.

Cling film can be used to cover dishes but do not allow it to touch the food. Pierce it or turn back a small area, to allow steam to escape during cooking.

Kitchen paper, greaseproof paper, microwave paper and non-stick baking paper are useful for wrapping or covering foods. Microwave and non-stick paper are ideal for lining dishes too. Don't use recycled kitchen paper – it can have minute traces of metal in it.

Useful accessories
A *microwave rack* is handy to encourage even cooking of all foods – to raise dishes in the cooker so that the microwaves can easily reach the food from every direction. They are also useful for thawing meat and other foods, preventing them from sitting in a pool of liquid.

Browning dishes are useful in microwave cookers. They have a special coating which heats up in the microwave, for searing and browning small items such as bacon, sausages, steaks, chops, eggs, fish, vegetables and toasted sandwiches. The surface of a browning dish can reach a temperature of up to 300°C(600°F) so always use oven gloves, follow the dish manufacturer's instructions carefully and never exceed the recommended pre-heating time. Once the food is put on to the hot surface, cooking is completed by microwaving.

A *plate ring* is useful for stacking plated meals for thawing or reheating in the microwave. You only need one because best results are obtained if no more than two plates are stacked.

4

Using Your Microwave

A microwave cooker is versatile – thawing, cooking and reheating food at a moment's notice. As you get to know your microwave, you will discover that several things affect thawing/cooking/reheating times and the way the microwave performs generally:

● the type of food, its moisture content (the more it contains, the longer it takes to cook) and its density (dense foods like meat take longer to thaw than porous foods such as bread and cake);

● the quantity of food – two potatoes take longer to cook than one, though not necessarily double the time – for this reason, avoid filling the microwave with food;

● its shape and size – regular shapes cook more evenly than irregular shapes, and small pieces cook quicker than large pieces;

● the starting temperature of the food dictates how long it takes to thaw/cook/reheat – for instance, food from the refrigerator takes longer to cook than food at room temperature;

● the container used – and its shape in particular – a circular shape with straight sides is best (see page 24);

● the power level used – the higher the power level the

faster the cooking;

- the way in which a food is cooked conventionally – food which normally requires slow, gentle cooking will usually benefit from cooking on a low power level in the microwave;

- the arrangement of the food – even layers encourage even heating; arrange individual foods in a circle with thicker areas towards the edge of the dish;

- turning, stirring and repositioning foods encourage even results too;

- the standing time – most foods should be allowed to stand for a short time after microwaving – to allow the temperature to even out and to allow the food to finish thawing, cooking or reheating.

THAWING

A microwave and a freezer make a good partnership. Food which normally takes hours to thaw out can be taken from the freezer and thawed in the microwave in a matter of minutes.

Food is thawed using the DEFROST or MEDIUM-LOW (30%) setting. The food is subjected to microwave energy in short bursts for about 30% of the time period (in some cookers it is possible to hear the energy switching on and off as it pulsates into the oven). By controlling the microwaves in this way, the food thaws slowly and evenly – during the period when no microwaves are entering the cavity, heat from the thawed areas is conducted to the colder areas. If the microwaves were not controlled, the food would thaw too quickly around the edges, heating up while the centre remained frozen solid.

After thawing, food should be allowed to stand for a short period, to allow any remaining ice crystals to disappear and to allow the temperature of the food to even out.

Many microwave cookers have an AUTO-DEFROST setting, which thaws food even more gently and incorporates a standing time too. Some models are controlled by time, during which the oven (which starts thawing on a fairly high power) gradually reduces the power level to LOW (10%). Some are controlled by the weight of the food – you simply program in the type and weight of food to be thawed, and the microwave does the rest. Others have a sensor which weighs the food and automatically calculates the thawing time.

HANDY HINTS – THAWING

● Frozen vegetables need no thawing – they can be cooked straight from the freezer.

● Containers which can be taken from freezer to microwave are the most convenient to use.

● If you don't want a container to stay, out of use, in the freezer, simply line it with foil or a freezer bag before adding the food, freezing it, and then lifting out the frozen block. Before thawing, just peel off the foil or freezer bag and replace the frozen food in its dish.

● Freeze food in shallow blocks – for quick and even thawing.

● Put a block of frozen food into a close-fitting dish for thawing – to prevent thawed areas spreading over the base of the dish and heating up too soon.

● Before thawing, remove any excess ice which may be

attached to food.

- Remove any metal ties, foil or foil containers before thawing.

- Open containers and bags of food before thawing – to prevent them splitting when the air inside heats and expands during thawing.

- Cover most food during thawing – to encourage even thawing in the minimum time. Baked foods, such as cakes, bread and pastries are best left uncovered – to prevent their surfaces from becoming too moist.

- Put cakes, bread and pastries on a sheet of absorbent kitchen paper – to soak up excess moisture during thawing.

- Arrange individual items in a circle, leaving the centre free, for even results.

- Follow the thawing times given in your manufacturer's instruction book until you are familiar with your microwave.

- Turn and reposition large or dense foods at least once during thawing.

- Separate foods as they thaw (such as sausages, chops and fish fillets) to encourage even thawing. Break up blocks of food (such as sauces and soups) as they soften.

- Should any part of the food begin to feel warm, stop thawing and allow it to stand for several minutes before starting again.

- Ensure poultry and meat are completely thawed before cooking.

REHEATING

A microwave reheats food in a fraction of the time it normally takes in the conventional oven or on the hob. Even foods which can be difficult to reheat (like pasta and rice) taste just as if they were freshly cooked. Some foods even improve with reheating, like casseroles and sauces.

HANDY HINTS – REHEATING

● When heating pre-packed ready-cooked foods, always follow the pack instructions carefully.

● If you freeze foods which have been bought from the fresh or chilled counters, remember that they should be thoroughly thawed before following the heating instructions on the packet. It's worth fixing a note to them so that other members of the household will remember too.

● Remove metal ties and transfer food from foil containers before reheating (unless the product and its container is specifically designed for the microwave).

● Chilled (refrigerated) food takes longer to reheat than food at room temperature (such as just-cooled food or cans of food from the store cupboard).

● Avoid reheating large items such as joints of meat. They tend to overcook and dry out before the centre is piping hot. Small pieces (e.g. meat slices) reheat more successfully.

● Arrange food in a shallow even layer whenever possible. A plated meal should be arranged in an even layer with thick, solid pieces toward the outer edge of the plate.

- Make a well in the centre of large quantities of food such as rice, pasta or vegetables, to encourage quick and even heating.

- Cover most foods during reheating, to keep in the heat and moisture. Use a lid with a vent when possible. Alternatively use pierced cling film. There are some exceptions to this rule, however. Putting a cover on very small quantities would be a hindrance; while bread, pastry, crumble toppings and any foods which need to stay dry, need no cover.

- Some foods are best reheated on HIGH (100%) while others are better on MEDIUM-HIGH (75%), MEDIUM (50%) or even MEDIUM-LOW (30%). Generally, delicate foods, large amounts and foods which tend to heat up extremely quickly in the microwave (mince pies, for example) are best reheated on a lower power. Check the charts for guidance.

- Stir or turn foods during reheating. When possible, stir before serving too.

- Avoid overheating, and therefore spoiling, foods. Pastry and crunchy toppings quickly lose their crispness if overheated. It's preferable to under estimate the heating time, then add extra if necessary.

- The first time you reheat a food, make a note of the time it takes – for future reference.

- Reheated food must be piping hot throughout.

- A food thermometer is useful to check the temperature of foods which are unsuitable for stirring.

- Leave food to stand for a short time after reheating – to allow the temperature to even out. Some foods (mince/fruit pies and baby food in particular) need careful checking before serving – to prevent burning.

Food	Amount	Reheat for:	Use:	Method and special instructions
Baby food	128g jar	30 secs	HIGH (100%)	Empty into a small serving bowl. Stir well once or twice during heating. Before serving, carefully check the temperature.
Baby milk	100ml (4 fl oz)	20-30 secs	HIGH (100%)	Stir or shake the milk well and pour into a sterilised bottle. Before serving, shake well and carefully check the temperature.
	225ml (8 fl oz)	40-50 secs		
Baked beans	220g can	1½ mins	HIGH (100%)	Empty into a shallow dish and cover. Stir once or twice during heating and again before serving.
	425g can	3-3½ mins		
Bread rolls	1-2	30-40 secs	MEDIUM (50%)	Arrange in a circle and in a single layer on paper towel.
	3-4	1 min		
	5-6	1-1½ mins		

Food	Amount	Reheat for:	Use:	Method and special instructions
Casserole-type dishes	1-2 servings	3-5 mins	HIGH (100%)	Put into a large casserole and cover. Stir occasionally during heating and again before serving.
	Family-size serving	9-12 mins		
Cornish pasty	1	½-1 min	MEDIUM (50%)	Put on microwave rack or pre-heated browning dish. Leave to stand for 2 mins before serving.
	2	1-1½ mins		
Cottage Pie - see *Shepherd's Pie*				
Christmas Pudding	1 serving	1 min	MEDIUM (50%)	Put in a serving dish. Do not overheat. Leave to stand for 1 min before serving.
	450g (1 lb)	3-5 mins		Put into a bowl and cover. Do not overheat. Leave to stand for 3-5 mins before serving.
	900g (2 lb)	8-12 mins		
Custard	150ml (¼ pt)	1-1½ mins	HIGH (100%)	Pour into a jug or bowl. Stir once during heating and again before serving.
	300ml (½ pt)	2-3 mins		
	600ml (1 pt)	3-4 mins		
Flan/quiche	1 serving	½-1 min	MEDIUM (50%)	Put on a serving plate or pre-heated browning dish. Leave to stand for 1-2 mins before serving.
	Family-size serving	3½-5 mins		

33

Food	Amount	Reheat for:	Use:	Method and special instructions
Fruit, cooked	1 serving	1-2 mins	MEDIUM (50%)	Put into a serving bowl and cover. Stir or rearrange once or twice during heating.
	2 servings	2-3 mins		
	4 servings	6 mins		
Fruit Crumble	1 serving	1 min	HIGH (100%)	Put into a serving bowl, uncovered. Leave to stand for 1-2 mins before serving.
	Family-size serving	6-9 mins	MEDIUM (50%)	
Fruit Pie	Individual	½-1 min	HIGH (100%)	Put on a microwave rack and pierce the pastry lid with a knife before heating. Leave to stand for 2 (individual) – 4 (family-size) mins before serving.
	Family-size	2-3 mins	MEDIUM (50%)	
Lasagne/ moussaka	1 serving	4-6 mins	MEDIUM (50%)	Pierce in several places with a sharp knife before heating. Leave to stand for 3-4 mins.
	Family-size serving	15-20 mins		
Mince Pies	2	30-50 secs	MEDIUM (50%)	Put on a microwave rack and pierce the pastry lids with a knife before heating. Leave to stand for 1-2 minutes before serving.
	4	1-2 mins		
	6	2-2½ mins		
Moussaka - see *Lasagne*				

Food	Amount		Reheat for:	Use:	Method and special instructions
Pasta, cooked	1 serving		1-1½ mins	HIGH (100%)	Put into a serving dish, add a little oil, butter or water and cover. Stir gently once or twice during heating.
	2 servings		1½-2 mins		
	4 servings		2½-3½ mins		
Pies: fish, meat and poultry. See also Fruit Pie and Mince Pies	Individual		½-1½ mins	HIGH (100%)	Put on a microwave rack and pierce the pastry lid with a sharp knife before heating. Leave to stand for 2 (individual) – 4 (family-size) mins before serving.
	Family-size		5-7 mins		
Pizza	Individual		1½-2½ mins	HIGH (100%)	Best results are obtained on a pre-heated browning dish.
	Large		3-5 mins		
Plated meal	1		3-4 mins	MEDIUM-HIGH (75%)	Cover. When heating 2 plates, use a plate ring to separate them and rearrange the plates half way. Leave to stand for 2-3 mins before serving.
	2		4-6 mins		
Potatoes, whole, cooked	1		1-2 mins	HIGH (100%)	Put on paper towel. Pierce skins in several places. Leave to stand for 2-3 mins before serving.
	2		2-3 mins		
	4		3-5 mins		

Food	Amount	Reheat for:	Use:	Method and special instructions
Potatoes, mashed	1 serving	30-50 secs	HIGH (100%)	Put into a dish and cover. Stir once or twice during heating. Leave to stand for 1-2 mins before serving.
	2 servings	1 min		
	4 servings	1½-2½ mins		
Quiche - see *Flan*				
Rice, cooked	1 serving	1 min	HIGH (100%)	Put into a dish and cover. Stir once or twice during heating and again before serving.
	2 servings	1½-2½ mins		
	4 servings	3-4 mins		
Rice pudding	1 serving	1-1½ mins	HIGH (100%)	Put into a bowl and cover. Stir once or twice during heating and again before serving.
	2 servings	2-3½ mins		
	4 servings	4-5 mins		
Sauce: meat e.g. bolognese	300ml (½ pt)	4-5 mins	HIGH (100%)	Pour into a jug or bowl. Stir once or twice during heating and again before serving.
	600ml (1 pt)	8-10 mins		
Sauce: tomato	300ml (½ pt)	3-4 mins	HIGH (100%)	Pour into a jug or bowl. Stir once or twice during heating and again before serving.
	600ml (1 pt)	5-7 mins		

Food	Amount	Reheat for:	Use:	Method and special instructions
Sauce: white	300ml (½ pt)	2-3 mins	HIGH (100%)	Pour into a jug or bowl. Stir once or twice during heating and again before serving.
	600ml (1 pt)	4-5 mins		
butterscotch	150ml (¼ pt)	1-1½ mins		
	300ml (½ pt)	2-3 mins		
chocolate	150ml (¼ pt)	1-1½ mins		
	300ml (½ pt)	2-3 mins		
Sausage rolls	2	20-30 secs	MEDIUM-HIGH (75%)	Put on a microwave rack or pre-heated browning dish. Leave to stand for 2 mins before serving. The top pastry will not be crisp.
	4	30-50 secs		
	6	1-1½ mins		
Shepherd's Pie	Individual	3-5 mins	MEDIUM (50%)	Pierce in several places with a sharp knife before heating. Leave to stand for 2 (individual) – 5 (family-size) mins before serving.
	Family-size	12-15 mins		

Food	Amount	Reheat for:	Use:	Method and special instructions
Soup	1 bowl	1½-2 mins	HIGH (100%)	Pour into individual bowls or a jug. Stir once or twice during heating and again before serving.
	2 bowls	2-2½ mins		
	600ml (1 pt)	6-7 mins		
Sponge pudding	1 serving	30-40 secs	MEDIUM-HIGH (75%)	Put in an individual serving dish and cover, or turn out a whole pudding on to a plate and cover with an upturned bowl. Do not overheat. Leave to stand for 1-2 mins before serving.
	Whole: 2-4 servings	2-3 mins		
Steak & kidney pudding	Individual	3-4 mins	MEDIUM (50%)	Turn on to a plate and cover with an upturned bowl. Do not overheat. Leave to stand for 2-3 mins before serving.
	large: 2-4 servings	8-10 mins		
Vegetables, leaf e.g. cabbage	1 serving	20-30 secs	HIGH (100%)	Put into a dish and cover. Stir once or twice during heating and again before serving.
	2 servings	40-50 secs		
	4 servings	1-1½ mins		
Vegetables, root e.g. carrots	1 serving	40-50 secs	HIGH (100%)	Put into a dish and cover. Stir once or twice during heating and again before serving.
	2 servings	1-1½ mins		
	4 servings	2-3 mins		

ADAPTING YOUR OWN RECIPES FOR MICROWAVE COOKING

Many of your everyday conventional recipes will be suitable for cooking in the microwave. With a little practice you will soon gain confidence, learning which will work and which won't.

HANDY HINTS

● Reduce the cooking time of your recipe to about one quarter to one third of the time it would take to cook conventionally.

● When trying out a recipe for the first time, always under-estimate the cooking time and check the cooking progress frequently. Remember that under-cooked food can usually be put back in the microwave for longer cooking, but over-cooked food is usually spoiled.

● Compare your recipe with a similar one in your microwave's instruction/cook book and in this book too. This way, you will get a feeling for which recipes will work and a guide to how long they will take to cook.

● Follow the hints on page 26.

● The fat content of a conventional recipe can often be reduced. Sometimes it's possible to cook recipes (soups and casseroles, for instance) with no additional fat.

● Use less salt and spicy seasonings during cooking. Flavours are often intensified in the microwave, so it's preferable to adjust the seasoning after cooking, before serving.

● Choose your power level with care. Check with similar

recipes in this book. If in doubt, then it's probably better to err on the side of caution and use a power level lower than HIGH (100%).

- Replace long-cooking ingredients with quick-cooking alternatives where it's convenient – canned beans instead of dried, for example.

- Stir or cover foods which you would normally stir or cover during conventional cooking.

- Always add delicate or quick-cooking ingredients to a recipe towards the end of cooking.

- Make sure that the cooked dish is piping hot throughout.

- When doubling recipe quantities, increase the (microwave) cooking time by about one quarter to one third.

- When halving recipe quantities, reduce the (microwave) cooking time by about one third.

LOOKING AFTER YOUR MICROWAVE

Look after your microwave, following the manufacturer's instructions, and it will reward you with years of reliable service. Avoid operating the microwave while it is empty – make sure by keeping a small container of water in the cavity in case someone accidentally switches it on. Do not use metal containers (unless the manufacturer allows this), do not allow anything to jam in the door (tea towels, for instance) and never lean heavily on the door. Lastly, make sure that every member of the household knows how to operate the microwave correctly.

Keeping a microwave cooker clean is usually a simple matter of wiping out the cavity after each use. The walls don't heat up during cooking, so food doesn't bake on them as it would in a conventional oven. This is not the case, however, with a combination cooker which does heat up – because the cavity is smaller than a conventional oven and the walls are closer to the cooking food, splashes can easily burn on.

HANDY HINTS – CLEANING

● Wipe out the interior frequently and regularly.

● Mop up spills and splashes as soon as they occur – spilled food and splashes will only slow down the cooking the next time the microwave is used.

● Removable parts, such as a turntable or a shelf, should be washed with hot water and detergent, then thoroughly dried.

● If the cavity walls become heavily soiled, put a bowl of water in the microwave and cook on HIGH (100%) until it boils – the steam produced will help to soften stubborn marks, which can then be wiped away with a soft cloth.

● To remove lingering odours from the oven, add some lemon slices to the bowl of water.

● Do not use abrasive cleaners on any part of a microwave or combination cooker, and never use a knife to clean off a stubborn mark.

● Never allow water or cleaning materials to enter any vents in the cavity.

● To clean stubborn stains from a combination cooker,

use liquid cleaners only. Look for specially-designed microwave cooker cleaners too.

Replacement parts

In the event that an oven part needs replacing (such as a turntable, shelf or bulb), obtain it from an authorised service agent. To find out your nearest one, contact the manufacturer of your microwave (the address and telephone number should be in your instruction book).

If a fault occurs

Always obtain qualified help – from a service engineer who has been authorised by your microwave manufacturer. Never remove the outer casing of the cooker or attempt to repair a fault yourself.

Servicing

If you use your microwave correctly and do not move it around frequently or drop it, there's little need to have it checked. However, if you have reason to believe that the microwave has been damaged in any way, or if you notice a change in its performance, you may wish to have it checked by an authorised engineer.

Many manufacturers offer a service contract on new ovens.

Leakage testing

If you look after your microwave, there is little need to have it checked. Were a microwave cooker to be damaged sufficiently (by dropping it, for instance) to allow leakage, it would not work. However, over the years many people have spoken to me, simply *wondering* whether their microwave cooker leaks. My answer is always reassuring, but I also understand that once doubts are installed in the mind, mistrust can linger. In these instances, I suggest that it may be worth putting their mind at ease by having the microwave checked over by a qualified engineer.

In the past, microwave owners have been tempted to buy low-cost hand-held leakage testers, which all proved to be unreliable. At the time of publication, there is still nothing as dependable as the costly machines used by authorised engineers and environmental health officers. Their leakage testers are recalibrated regularly so you can be sure that they are accurate.

5

About The Recipes

● The recipes in this book have been tested in 600-700W microwave cookers. If your microwave has a higher wattage, you can either reduce the cooking times on HIGH (100%) slightly (by about 25%) or simply use a lower power level which is the equivalent of 600-700W and cook for the recommended time. If your microwave is less than 600W, you will need to increase the cooking times by about 30%.

● All cooking is on HIGH (100%) unless otherwise stated.

● When it is important to cover (or not) during cooking, the method states this. If no instruction is given, then it makes little difference whether you cover the food or not.

● In cookers without turntables, food may need turning or repositioning occasionally.

● Each recipe starts with the number of servings and an approximate cooking time. The ❊ symbol indicates that the dish is suitable for freezing.

● When a recipe benefits from using a grill, this is also indicated at the start of the recipe. Grilling can take place in the microwave, if your model has one, or under a conventional grill, if it doesn't.

- Ingredients are given in metric and imperial. Follow one type of measure for successful results.

- Spoon quantities are level unless otherwise stated.

- Flour is plain and eggs are size 3 unless otherwise stated.

Combination cookers
There are no recipes for combination cooking (that is, using conventional oven heat together with microwaves) in this book. Combination cookers still vary tremendously in the way they operate, making it difficult to give recipes which are guaranteed to work in every model. Best results are usually obtained by first following the manufacturer's instructions and recipes, then experimenting with your own recipes once you get to know the cooker and how it performs.

6

Soups and Starters

Home-made soups are quick and easy in the microwave, whether you are making an individual portion or enough for a family.

Those of us who still like to make the occasional pot of home-made stock find it convenient to put the broken-up bones, chicken carcass or well-washed vegetable peelings into a bowl, cover them with water, bring to the boil on HIGH (100%) and cook on MEDIUM-LOW (30%) for about 30 minutes. When the mixture is strained, you have a delicious fresh stock ready for adding to sauces and, in particular, to soups.

HANDY HINTS – SOUPS

● Use a large, deep bowl so that the soup has plenty of room to boil up. This is particularly important where milk is an ingredient.

- If you are adapting a conventional soup recipe for the microwave, reduce the liquid by about one quarter. There is usually less evaporation in the microwave. If the finished soup is too thick, it can always be diluted after cooking.

- Cut ingredients such as vegetables into even pieces to encourage even cooking. The smaller they are cut, the quicker they will cook.

- Speed up the cooking time by adding *boiling* water or stock to the main ingredients (an electric kettle boils a large quantity of water more efficiently than a microwave). To speed up cooking even further use only half the liquid, then add the extra (hot) after cooking.

- Cover soup to keep the moisture and heat in. A lid with a vent helps to prevent it boiling over. If you don't have a vented lid, put a wooden cocktail stick between the bowl and lid.

- Most soups can be cooked on HIGH (100%). Remember, the cooking time will depend on the ingredient with the longest cooking time.

- If a soup contains meat which requires tenderising, rice, pasta or other cereals, it will cook just as quickly if it is first brought to the boil on HIGH (100%), then cooked on MEDIUM (50%) or MEDIUM-LOW (30%) for the remaining time.

  In the same way, a soup can be left to simmer gently, to develop its flavour, just as you would leave it on the hob.

- Stir the soup occasionally during cooking.

- *Dried soup:* Whisk the soup mix with hot water (from the kettle) following the packet instructions. Cook on

HIGH (100%), stirring occasionally, until the soup boils, then lower the power to MEDIUM (50%) or MEDIUM-LOW (30%), cover and cook for the time stated on the packet, stirring occasionally.

● *Cans and cartons of soup:* Pour the soup into a bowl or jug, diluting it according to label instructions if necessary. Cover and cook on HIGH (100%), stirring occasionally, until hot.

FRESH TOMATO SOUP

Serves 4-6

Cooking time: 25 mins

❄

25g (1 oz) butter
1 lean bacon rasher, rind removed and finely chopped
1 medium onion, finely chopped
1 carrot, finely chopped
10ml (2 tsp) sugar
450g (1 lb) fresh tomatoes, chopped; or
 400g can chopped tomatoes
450ml (³/₄ pt) boiling chicken stock
salt and freshly ground black pepper
bouquet garni
10ml (2 tsp) lemon juice
30ml (2 tbsp) tomato purée
chopped parsley, to serve
croûtons or crusty bread, to serve

1. Put the butter, bacon, onion, carrot and sugar in a large bowl. Cover and cook for 5 mins, stirring once.

2. Add the remaining ingredients, except the parsley and bread. Cover and cook for 20 mins, stirring occasionally.

3. Leave the soup to stand for 10 mins then remove the bouquet garni.

4. Purée the soup in a blender or food processor. For a really smooth soup, strain through a sieve after puréeing.

5. Reheat if necessary. Sprinkle with chopped parsley and serve with croûtons or crusty bread.

CREAM OF TOMATO SOUP

Follow method for FRESH TOMATO SOUP and stir in 150ml (¹/₄ pt) single or double cream before serving.

TOMATO AND VEGETABLE SOUP

Serves 6

Cooking time: about 20 mins

❋

450g (1 lb) ripe tomatoes, quartered
1 large potato, finely chopped
2 medium leeks, thinly sliced
1 small carrot, thinly sliced
750ml (1¼ pt) chicken stock
5ml (1 tsp) Worcestershire sauce
salt and freshly ground black pepper
45ml (3 tbsp) tomato purée
60ml (4 tbsp) single cream

1. Put the tomatoes, potato, leeks and carrot into a large bowl. Add 150ml (¼ pt) stock, Worcestershire sauce and seasoning. Cover and cook for about 15 minutes, stirring occasionally.

2. Stir in the remaining stock and the tomato purée. Tip the soup into a blender or food processor and purée until smooth.

3. Pass the soup through a nylon sieve, to remove skin and seeds. Adjust seasoning if necessary.

4. Reheat for about 5 minutes, stirring once.

5. Stir in the cream just before serving.

FRENCH ONION SOUP

Serves 4-6

Cooking time: about 27 mins

❊ *omit the bread and cheese*

40g (1½ oz) butter
450g (1 lb) onions, finely sliced
1 garlic clove, crushed
5ml (1 tsp) sugar
600ml (1 pt) boiling beef stock
15ml (1 tbsp) Worcestershire sauce
salt and freshly ground black pepper
4 slices of French bread
75g (3 oz) Cheddar or Gruyère cheese, grated

1. Put the butter, onions, garlic and sugar in a large bowl, cover and cook for 5 mins, stirring once.

2. Add the boiling stock, Worcestershire sauce and seasoning. Cover and cook for 15-20 mins, stirring occasionally.

3. Arrange the bread slices on a plate and top with the cheese. Cook, uncovered, for 1-2 mins until the cheese has melted. Float them on top of the soup, to serve.

   Alternatively, pour the soup into a warmed flameproof casserole, float the bread slices on top, sprinkle with cheese and cook under a hot grill until the cheese bubbles.

CREAM OF ONION SOUP

Follow stages 1-2 for FRENCH ONION SOUP, then purée in a blender or food processor and stir in 150ml (¼pt) single cream. Omit the bread and cheese. Instead, fry some onion rings in butter or oil until crisp and brown, and scatter over the soup to serve.

MUSHROOM AND ONION SOUP

Serves 4-6

Cooking time: about 15 mins   ❊

40g (1¹/₂ oz) butter
450g (1 lb) onions, thinly sliced
600ml (1 pt) boiling beef or vegetable stock
15ml (1 tbsp) Worcestershire sauce
10ml (2 tsp) French mustard
125g (4 oz) mushrooms, finely chopped
salt and freshly ground black pepper

1. Put the butter and onions into a large bowl. Cover and cook for 5 mins, stirring once.

2. Stir in the remaining ingredients, cover and cook for about 10 mins, stirring once or twice.

3. Leave the soup to stand, covered, for 5-10 mins before serving.

CHICKEN AND VEGETABLE SOUP
Serves 4
Cooking time: about 35 mins
❄

chicken portion, weighing 175-225g (6-8 oz)
1 bay leaf
1 garlic clove
bouquet garni
1 small onion, finely chopped
1 medium carrot, diced
1 medium leek, finely sliced
1 celery stick, finely sliced
30ml (2 tbsp) Worcestershire sauce
salt and freshly ground black pepper

1. Put the chicken in a medium bowl with 300ml ($^1/_2$ pt) water, bay leaf, garlic and bouquet garni. Cover and cook for 20 mins. Leave to stand for 5 mins.

2. Meanwhile, put the onion, carrot, leek and celery into a large bowl, cover and cook for 5 mins, stirring once.

3. Lift the chicken out of its stock, remove and discard the skin and bones and chop the chicken meat into small pieces. Strain the stock, discarding the bay leaf, garlic and bouquet garni.

4. Add the chicken to the vegetables and pour the chicken stock over. Stir in the Worcestershire sauce, 150ml ($^1/_4$ pt) water and salt and pepper to taste.

5. Cover and cook for 10-15 mins, stirring occasionally, until the vegetables are tender.

CHINESE CHICKEN SOUP

Serves 4-6
Cooking time: about 20 mins ✳

25g (1 oz) butter
1 lean back bacon rasher, rind removed and chopped
175g (6 oz) chicken breast fillet, thinly sliced
6 spring onions, sliced
1.1 litre (2 pt) boiling chicken stock
100g (4 oz) button mushrooms, quartered
100g (4 oz) beansprouts
1.25ml (¼ tsp) dried mixed herbs
15ml (1 tbsp) soy sauce
salt and freshly ground black pepper

1. Put the butter and bacon into a large bowl, cover and cook for 3 minutes, stirring once.

2. Add the remaining ingredients, cover and cook for about 15 mins.

3. Allow the soup to stand for 10-15 mins before adjusting the seasoning and serving.

FROZEN VEGETABLE SOUP

Serves 4-6

Cooking time: about 30 mins

❄

1 medium onion, finely chopped
4 lean streaky bacon rashers, chopped
900ml (1½ pt) boiling chicken stock
1 medium potato, thinly sliced
45ml (3 tbsp) tomato purée
2.5ml (½ tsp) dried mixed herbs
225g (8 oz) frozen mixed vegetables
salt and freshly ground black pepper
grated Parmesan cheese

1. Put the onion and bacon in a large bowl, cover and cook for 5 minutes, stirring once.

2. Add the remaining ingredients, cover and cook for about 25 minutes, stirring occasionally.

3. Leave the soup to stand for 5-10 minutes before adjusting the seasoning.

4. Serve sprinkled with Parmesan cheese.

MINTED PEA SOUP

Serves 4

Cooking time: about 15 mins   ❄

1 bunch of spring onions
100g (4 oz) frozen peas
100g (4 oz) potatoes, diced
300ml (¹/₂ pt) vegetable stock
5ml (1 tsp) concentrated mint sauce
300ml (¹/₂ pt) milk
salt and freshly ground black pepper
150ml (¹/₄ pt) double cream

1. Trim and chop the spring onions, reserving some of the green tops for a garnish.

2. Put the onions, peas, potatoes and stock into a large bowl. Cover and cook for 10-15 mins, stirring once, until the vegetables are soft.

3. Leave to stand for 5 mins, then purée the soup in a blender or food processor. Stir in the mint sauce, milk and seasoning to taste.

4. Serve warm or chilled. Top each bowl of soup with a generous swirl of cream and scatter over the reserved onion tops.

LEEK AND POTATO SOUP

Cooking time: about 20 mins

25g (1 oz) butter
2 medium leeks, thinly sliced
1 medium onion, finely chopped
350g (12 oz) potatoes, finely sliced
600ml (1 pt) boiling chicken or vegetable stock
salt and freshly ground pepper
150ml (¼ pt) double cream
chopped chives, to serve

1. Put the butter, leeks and onion in a large bowl, cover and cook for 5 mins, stirring once.

2. Add the potatoes, boiling stock and seasoning. Cover and cook for 10-15 mins, stirring occasionally, until the vegetables are tender.

3. Purée the soup in a blender or food processor. Stir in the cream.

4. Reheat for 2-3 mins, without boiling.

5. Serve sprinkled with chives.

PARSNIP AND LEEK SOUP

Serves 4

Cooking time: about 15 mins

✳

225g (8 oz) parsnips, finely chopped or grated
225g (8 oz) leeks, thinly sliced
1 chicken stock cube
pinch of ground mace
salt and freshly ground pepper
450ml (³/₄ pt) milk
30ml (2 tbsp) snipped chives

1. Put the parsnips, leeks, crumbled stock cube and mace into a large bowl. Add 150ml (¹/₄ pt) water and season with salt and pepper. Cover and cook for 10 minutes, stirring once or twice.

2. Stir in the milk, tip into a blender or food processor and purée until smooth.

3. Reheat for 3-5 minutes.

4. Serve sprinkled with chives.

CREAMY BUTTER BEAN AND BACON SOUP

Cooking time: about 20 mins　　　　　　　*Serves 4-6*

❋ *omit cream and parsley*

25g (1 oz) butter
1 medium onion, finely chopped
4 lean bacon rashers, rinds removed and finely chopped
two 439g cans butter beans, drained
600ml (1 pt) boiling chicken stock
2.5ml (¹/₂ tsp) dried mixed herbs
salt and freshly ground black pepper
150ml (¹/₄ pt) single cream
chopped parsley, to serve

1. Put the butter, onion and bacon into a large bowl, cover and cook for 5 mins, stirring once.

2. Add the beans, boiling stock, herbs and seasoning. Cover and cook for about 15 mins, stirring occasionally.

3. Using a slotted spoon, lift out one or two spoonfuls of bean mixture and reserve. Purée the remaining soup in a blender or food processor and add the cream.

4. Return the soup to its bowl and add the reserved bean mixture. Reheat for 2-3 mins if necessary, without boiling.

5. Sprinkle with parsley to serve.

HADDOCK AND CORN CHOWDER   *Serves 4*
Cooking time: about 25 mins

450g (1 lb) smoked haddock
300ml (¹/₂ pt) vegetable stock
1 medium onion, finely chopped
15g (¹/₂ oz) butter
450g (1 lb) potatoes, diced
salt and freshly ground pepper
198g can sweetcorn
300ml (¹/₂ pt) milk

1. Put the haddock in a shallow dish and add the stock. Cover and cook for 5 mins. Leave to stand for 10 mins.

2. Meanwhile, put the onion and butter in a large bowl, cover and cook for 3 mins.

3. Lift the haddock from its dish, reserving the stock. Flake the fish, discarding skin and bones.

4. Add the potatoes and reserved fish stock to the onion. Cover and cook for 10-12 mins, stirring once, until the potatoes are tender. Season to taste.

5. Add the haddock, sweetcorn (no need to drain it) and milk. Reheat for 3-5 mins before serving. Do not let it boil.

SINGLE-SERVE LENTIL SOUP

Serves 1

Cooking time: about 30 mins   ❄

4 spring onions, sliced
1 medium carrot, finely chopped
1 lean bacon rasher, rind removed and chopped
300ml (¹/₂ pt) vegetable stock
pinch of ground cumin
25g (1 oz) lentils
salt and freshly ground black pepper
5ml (1 tsp) lemon juice

1. Put the onions, carrot and bacon into a bowl, cover and cook for 2 mins.

2. Stir in the remaining ingredients. Cook for about 3 mins or until boiling.

3. Cover and cook on MEDIUM (50%) for 20-30 mins or until the lentils are tender.

4. Pour into a blender or food processor and purée until smooth. Adjust the seasoning before serving and thin the soup with a little boiling water if necessary.

KIPPER PATE

Cooking time: about 9 mins

200g bag frozen, boned kipper fillets with butter
45ml (3 tbsp) double cream
15ml (1 tbsp) lemon juice
5ml (1 tsp) horseradish sauce
freshly ground black pepper

1. Pierce the upper side of the bag of kipper fillets and put it on a plate. Cook on MEDIUM (50%) for about 9 mins or until cooked.

2. Leave the kipper fillets to cool slightly, then cut the bag and let the fish and juices slide out on to the plate. Remove and discard the skin.

3. Put the fish and its juices into a blender or food processor. Add the cream, lemon juice and horseradish sauce and purée until smooth. Season with pepper.

4. Spoon into a dish, cover and chill.

CHICKEN LIVER PATE

Cooking time: about 11 mins

Serves 4-6

❄

25g (1 oz) butter
1 medium onion, finely chopped
1 large garlic clove, crushed
450g (1 lb) chicken livers
2 bay leaves
100g (4 oz) curd cheese
60ml (4 tbsp) Greek yoghurt
30ml (2 tbsp) dry sherry
few drops of hot pepper sauce
salt and freshly ground black pepper
parsley sprigs, to garnish
crusty bread, toast or biscuits, to serve

1. Put the butter, onion and garlic in a medium bowl, cover and cook for 3 mins.

2. Stir in the livers and bay leaves. Cook uncovered for 6-8 mins, stirring occasionally, until the livers are cooked.

3. Cover and leave to cool. Remove and discard the bay leaves.

4. Tip the liver mixture into a blender or food processor. Add the cheese, yoghurt, sherry and pepper sauce and purée until smooth. Season to taste, if wished. Spoon into a serving dish, cover and refrigerate.

5. Garnish with parsley and serve with crusty bread, toast or biscuits.

HOT GRAPEFRUIT WITH VERMOUTH *Serves 2*
Cooking time: about 2¹/₂ mins

1 grapefruit
10-20ml (2-4 tsp) sweet red vermouth
25g (1 oz) butter
30ml (2 tbsp) soft brown sugar
glacé cherries or orange slices

1. Halve the grapefruit and put into two dishes. Use a grapefruit knife or small sharp knife to cut around and loosen each segment. Sprinkle the vermouth over.

2. In a small bowl, melt the butter for 30 secs and brush over the grapefruit. Sprinkle with the sugar.

3. Cook both dishes together, uncovered, for about 2 mins until hot through.

4. Top with glacé cherries or orange slices and serve immediately.

PRUNE AND GRAPEFRUIT COMPOTE *Serves 2*
Cooking time: about 7 mins

50g (2 oz) ready-to-eat dried prunes
150ml (¹/₄ pt) apple juice
1 small grapefruit, peeled and cut into segments
icing sugar (optional)

1. Put the prunes and apple juice into a bowl, cover and cook for about 7 mins, stirring once.

2. Leave to cool, covered.

3. Stir in the grapefruit and sugar to taste. Chill until needed.

STUFFED MUSHROOMS
Cooking time: about 4 mins

Serves 4

40g (1¹/₂ oz) butter
50g (2 oz) fresh breadcrumbs
50g (2 oz) garlic sausage, finely chopped
50g (2 oz) Cheddar cheese, finely grated
15ml (1 tbsp) chopped parsley
5ml (1 tsp) pesto
beaten egg
salt and freshly ground black pepper
4 large flat mushrooms
parsley sprigs to garnish

1. Put 15g (¹/₂ oz) butter in a medium bowl and cook for 30 secs until melted. Stir in the breadcrumbs, sausage, cheese, parsley and pesto. Add sufficient beaten egg to bind the mixture. Season to taste.

2. Remove the stalks from the mushrooms, chop finely and add to the breadcrumb mixture. Spoon into the mushrooms and dot with the remaining butter.

3. Cover and cook for 3-4 mins. Garnish with parsley to serve.

GARLIC MUSHROOMS

Serves 4

Cooking time: about 5 mins

25g (1 oz) butter

1 garlic clove, crushed

225g (8 oz) small button mushrooms

salt and freshly ground black pepper

15ml (1 tbsp) white wine vinegar

30ml (2 tbsp) chopped parsley

toast triangles, to serve

1. Put the butter and garlic in a bowl and cook for $\frac{1}{2}$-1 min until the butter has melted.

2. Stir in the mushrooms, coating them with the butter. Season lightly and add the vinegar. Cover and cook for 3-4 mins, stirring once or twice.

3. Stir in the parsley and serve immediately with toast.

HOT COURGETTE AND TOMATO SALAD

Cooking time: 5-6 mins

Serves 2

1 garlic clove

25g (1 oz) fresh breadcrumbs

2 small courgettes

2 medium tomatoes, sliced

30ml (2 tbsp) French salad dressing

1. Halve the garlic clove and rub the cut sides around the inside of a small ovenproof dish. Add the breadcrumbs and cook for 1-2 mins, stirring frequently, until crisp and golden brown. Leave to stand.

2. Use a potato peeler to cut the courgettes lengthways into long ribbons. Arrange them on two small plates with the tomatoes. Sprinkle the dressing over them.

3. Cover and cook each plate for 2 mins (or both plates for about 3 mins), turning them half way through cooking. Top with the crisp crumbs; serve immediately.

SPINACH SALAD WITH HOT BACON DRESSING
Serves 4

Cooking time: about 6 mins

225g (8 oz) fresh young spinach leaves
225g (8 oz) bacon rashers, rinds removed and chopped
30ml (2 tbsp) oil
4 spring onions, finely chopped
15ml (1 tbsp) white wine or cider vinegar
5ml (1 tsp) soft brown sugar
15ml (1 tbsp) wholegrain mustard
salt and freshly ground black pepper

1. Wash, trim and dry the spinach, shredding any large leaves. Arrange in a serving bowl.

2. Put the bacon in a medium bowl and cook, uncovered, for about 5 mins, stirring occasionally, until it begins to brown and crisp. Add the remaining ingredients and cook for 1 min.

3. Pour the bacon dressing over the spinach and serve immediately.

SMOKED HAM AND EGG RAMEKINS
Serves 2

Cooking time: about 2 mins

1 slice of smoked ham
2 eggs (at room temperature)
salt and freshly ground black pepper
30ml (2 tbsp) Greek yoghurt
paprika

1. Halve the ham and place each piece in a ramekin dish. Break an egg into each and prick the yolks. Add a little seasoning and spoon the yoghurt over.

2. Cook, uncovered, on MEDIUM (50%) for about 2 mins or until the eggs are nearly set. Leave to stand for 1-2 mins to finish setting.

3. Sprinkle with paprika and serve immediately.

PASTA IN TOMATO, TUNA AND WINE SAUCE

Cooking time: about 23 mins *Serves 4*

❄ *sauce and pasta separately*

1 medium onion, finely chopped
2 garlic cloves, crushed
400g can chopped tomatoes
150ml (1/4 pt) dry white vermouth
1 vegetable stock cube
175g (6 oz) pasta shapes, such as twists or shells
198g can tuna, drained and flaked
freshly ground black pepper
30ml (2 tbsp) chopped fresh herbs, such as basil, oregano or fennel

1. Put the onion and garlic into a medium bowl, cover and cook for 3 mins.
2. Stir in the tomatoes, vermouth and crumbled stock cube. Cover and cook for 10 mins, stirring occasionally.
3. Put the pasta in a large bowl and cover well with boiling water. Cook, uncovered, for 8 mins, stirring once or twice. Leave to stand for 5 mins.
4. Meanwhile, add the tuna, pepper and herbs to the tomato sauce, cover and cook for 2-3 mins until hot.
5. Drain the pasta and serve it topped with, or tossed in, the sauce.

LEMON SOLE WITH SMOKED SALMON

Cooking time: about 5 mins   *Serves 2*

2 lemon sole fillets, skinned
50g (2 oz) smoked salmon slices
30ml (2 tbsp) dry white vermouth
45ml (3 tbsp) double cream
5ml (1 tsp) cornflour
2 spring onions, finely chopped
salt and freshly ground pepper
squeeze of lemon or lime juice
15ml (1 tbsp) finely chopped parsley

1. Cut each sole fillet in half lengthways. Put a strip of smoked salmon on the skinned side of each piece of sole. Roll each from its widest end and secure with a wooden cocktail stick.

2. Arrange the fish around the edge of a small shallow dish and add the vermouth. Cover and cook for about 2 mins until the fish is just cooked.

3. Carefully pour the liquid from around the fish into a jug. Whisk in the cream and cornflour, then add the onions. Cook for 2-3 mins, stirring frequently, until the sauce thickens and boils. Season to taste and stir in the lemon or lime juice and parsley.

4. Serve the fish with the sauce.

7
Fish

Fish is made for the microwave! It cooks quickly, keeps its shape beautifully and retains all its juices. Cook it whole or in fillets; just as it is, brushed with butter, or in a sauce. No matter which method you choose, so long as you don't overcook it, the texture and taste are wonderful.

HANDY HINTS – THAWING

● Thaw fish on DEFROST or MEDIUM-LOW (30%).

● Cover it to ensure even thawing.

● Separate pieces and reposition them as they begin to thaw.

● Take care not to overheat it or the fish will start to cook around the edges. If any areas start to feel warm, stop thawing and leave the fish to stand for 5-10 mins before continuing.

Guide to thawing times	
on DEFROST or MEDIUM-LOW (30%)	
Whole round fish	4-6 mins per 450g (1 lb)
Whole flat fish	3-4 mins per 450g (1 lb)
Cutlets, steaks and fillets	3-4 mins per 450g (1 lb)
Prawns and shrimps	2-3 mins per 100g (4 oz)
	3-4 mins per 225g (8 oz)
Scallops	3-4 mins per 225g (8 oz)

HANDY HINTS – COOKING

● Make a few slits in the skin of whole fish. This allows steam to escape and prevents the skin from bursting open.

● Use a shallow dish, unless you are cooking fish in a sauce, casserole or soup.

● Arrange fish in an even layer to encourage it to cook evenly. When cooking whole fish, overlap their tails, or lay them side by side with head to tail. With fillets, either roll them up and secure each with a wooden cocktail stick, or tuck the thin ends underneath the thick ends to achieve an even layer. When cooking fish steaks, arrange them with the thinner ends towards the centre of the dish.

- Season with salt after cooking to prevent the fish drying out and the surface from toughening.

- When cooking with butter, best results are achieved if it is melted first and brushed over the fish.

- Cover during cooking to keep the moisture in.

- Turn whole fish once during cooking.

- Take care not to overcook fish. Shellfish cooks especially quickly and is easily overcooked – for this reason add it to a dish towards the end of cooking.

- Should you find that fish easily overcooks on HIGH (100%), try using a lower power level and cooking for slightly longer.

- Check that fish is cooked by lifting up the flakes with a fork. If it is still slightly undercooked, just lay the flakes back down again and allow the fish to stand and the temperature to even out – the flakes should turn opaque and cook to perfection.

- Leave cooked fish to stand for a minute or two before serving.

- *Boil-in-the-bag* fish can be cooked in its bag. Remember to pierce the bag before cooking.

- *Fish in breadcrumbs or batter* is generally not suitable for microwave cooking, though fish fingers are acceptable when cooked on a browning dish (follow the dish manufacturer's instructions).

Guide to cooking times	
Per 450g (1 lb) on HIGH (100%)	
Whole round fish	4 mins
Whole flat fish	3 mins
Steaks, cutlets and thick fillets	4-6 mins
Thin fillets	2-3 mins
Prawns, raw	2-4 mins
Scallops, shelled	2-3 mins, adding corals for final 1-2 mins

If you find that fish cooked on HIGH (100%) tends to spit and overcook, try reducing the power to MEDIUM (50%) and cooking for a little longer.

FISH – Basic method

1. Put the fish in an even layer in a shallow dish. If wished, brush with melted butter or add 30ml (2 tbsp) water, stock, milk or wine.

2. Cover and cook, using the times above as a guide.

3. Leave to stand for 3-5 mins before serving.

MUSSELS – Basic method

1. Put 450-900g (1-2 lb) cleaned mussels in a large bowl. Add 150ml ($^1/_4$ pt) stock, wine or water and a little finely chopped onion and garlic.

2. Cover and cook for 3-5 mins, shaking the bowl occasionally and removing mussels from the top as they cook. Discard any that refuse to open. Use a slotted spoon to lift the mussels on to a warm serving dish.

3. Season the sauce with salt and freshly ground pepper, add some chopped fresh herbs and, if wished, stir in 45ml (3 tbsp) double cream. Cook on HIGH (100%) until boiling.

4. Pour the sauce over the mussels and serve.

PLAICE WITH LEMON SAUCE
Cooking time: about 6 mins

Serves 2

15g (¹/₂ oz) butter
4 plaice fillets, skinned
30ml (2 tbsp) chopped parsley
10ml (2 tsp) cornflour
grated rind and juice of half a lemon
45ml (3 tbsp) white wine
2.5ml (¹/₂ tsp) sugar
salt and freshly ground pepper

1. Heat the butter for 30 secs until melted and brush over the skinned side of each plaice fillet. Sprinkle the parsley over. Roll up the fillets from the thick end and arrange them in a shallow dish.

2. Cover and cook for 4 mins. Leave to stand for 3 mins.

3. Meanwhile, put the cornflour into a bowl or jug and whisk in the remaining ingredients. Carefully add any juices from around the fish.

4. Cook, uncovered, for 1-2 mins, stirring occasionally, until the sauce thickens and boils.

5. Pour the sauce over the fish and reheat for ¹/₂-1 min. Serve immediately.

PLAICE WITH ORANGE SAUCE
Follow the method for PLAICE WITH LEMON SAUCE, using orange rind and juice instead of lemon rind and juice.

PLAICE WITH CAPER BUTTER

Serves 1

Cooking time: about 4 mins

25g (1 oz) butter
15-25g ($^{1}/_{2}$-1 oz) capers, drained
5ml (1 tsp) chopped fresh parsley
freshly ground black pepper
1 large plaice fillet
5ml (1 tsp) lemon juice

1. Put the butter into a small dish and cook for about 30 secs or until melted. Stir in the capers and parsley. Season with pepper. Cover and cook for 30 secs.

2. Brush a little of the butter mixture over the base of a small shallow dish. Put the plaice in the dish and brush to coat it with the butter mixture. Cover and cook on MEDIUM-HIGH (75%) for about 2 mins or until the fish is just cooked.

3. Reheat the remaining butter mixture for 10-20 secs and pour it over the plaice. Sprinkle with lemon juice to serve.

TROUT WITH ALMONDS

Serves 2

Cooking time: about 8 mins

**2 trout, each weighing about 225g (8 oz), cleaned and
heads removed**
salt and freshly ground pepper
25g (1 oz) butter
25g (1 oz) flaked almonds
lemon wedges, to serve

1. Using a sharp knife, make two or three shallow slits in the skin on each side of the trout. Season inside with salt and pepper.

2. Heat half the butter for 30 secs until melted. Brush the trout with the butter then arrange, head to tail, in a shallow dish.

3. Cover and cook for about 4 mins or until just cooked, gently turning the fish over half way. Keep warm.

4. Meanwhile, put the remaining butter in an ovenproof dish and heat for 30 secs until melted. Stir in the almonds and cook for 2-3 mins, stirring frequently, until just golden brown.

5. Scatter the almonds and butter over the trout and serve immediately with lemon wedges.

FISH PIE

Serves 4

Cooking time: about 15 mins (plus white sauce & eggs)

white sauce, made with 600ml (1 pt) milk (page 92)
450g (1 lb) white or smoked fish (cod or haddock)
skinned, boned and cut into cubes
100g (4 oz) frozen peas
2 eggs, hard-boiled and shelled or baked (page 155)
and chopped
30ml (2 tbsp) chopped parsley
550g (1¼ lb) potatoes, sliced
milk
salt and freshly ground pepper

1. Into the hot white sauce, stir the fish, peas and parsley. Cover and cook for 3 mins, stirring once. Tip into a flameproof dish.

2. Put the potatoes into a large bowl with 60ml (4 tbsp) water. Cover and cook for about 8 mins or until the potatoes are tender, stirring occasionally. Mash the potatoes with a little milk and season to taste.

3. Spoon the potatoes on top of the fish mixture.

4. Either reheat, uncovered, for 3-5 minutes, or brown under a hot grill.

FISH IN PAPER PARCELS

Serves 4

Cooking time: about 10 mins

4 baby carrots, cut into thin matchsticks
4 spring onions, finely sliced
50g (2 oz) mushrooms, finely sliced
oil
4 fish steaks or fillets, such as cod, salmon or halibut,
each weighing about 175g (6 oz)
30ml (2 tbsp) chopped fresh herbs, such as dill, fennel
or parsley
salt and freshly ground pepper
50g (2 oz) butter

1. Put the carrots, onions and mushrooms in a small bowl, cover and cook for 4 mins, stirring once.

2. Meanwhile, cut four rectangles of greaseproof paper, each large enough to wrap one piece of fish generously. Brush one side of each sheet with a little oil.

3. Put a fish portion on the oiled side of each sheet of paper and top with the vegetables. Sprinkle over any liquid from the vegetables.

4. Blend the herbs and a little seasoning into the butter and top each pile of vegetables with one quarter of the butter.

5. Fold the paper over the fish and tuck the short ends underneath to form neat parcels. Arrange in a shallow dish.

6. Cook for about 6 mins or until the fish is just cooked. Leave to stand for 2-3 mins.

7. Serve the fish in the paper so each person can enjoy the delicious aroma as his/her parcel is opened.

FISH WITH SUMMER DRESSING   *Serves 4*
Cooking time: about 8 mins

**4 white fish fillets, such as cod or haddock, each
    weighing about 175g (6 oz)**
10ml (2 tsp) lemon juice or white wine vinegar
150g (5 oz) Greek yoghurt
2.5ml (½ tsp) concentrated mint sauce
**10cm (4 in) piece of cucumber, skinned, seeds removed
    and diced**
50g (2 oz) seedless green grapes, halved
salt and freshly ground pepper
thin cucumber slices, to garnish

1. Arrange the fish fillets in a shallow dish and sprinkle
   with the lemon juice or vinegar. Cover and cook for 5
   mins.

2. Mix together the yoghurt, mint sauce and cucumber.
   Reserve some grapes for garnish, then stir the
   remainder into the yoghurt mixture. Season lightly
   with salt and pepper. Spread the mixture evenly over
   the fish.

3. Cover and cook for a further 3 mins or until the fish is
   just cooked. Leave to stand for 2-3 mins.

4. Serve, garnished with cucumber slices and the
   reserved grapes.

FISH FLORENTINE

Serves 4

Cooking time: about 12 mins (plus white sauce)

450g (1 lb) fresh spinach
salt and freshly ground black pepper
25g (1 oz) butter
4 fish fillets (such as cod, haddock or smoked
    haddock), each weighing about 175g (6 oz)
white sauce, made with 300ml (¹/₂ pt) milk (page 92)
50g (2 oz) grated Cheddar cheese

1. Wash the spinach, shaking off the excess water. Put it into a large bowl, cover and cook for 4-5 mins, or until just tender. Drain thoroughly, squeezing out any excess liquid. Season with salt and pepper, stir in the butter and spoon into a serving dish. Keep warm.

2. Put the fish in a shallow dish, cover and cook for about 6 mins or until just cooked.

3. Arrange the fish on top of the spinach and stir any juices into the hot white sauce. Pour the sauce over the fish and sprinkle with the cheese.

4. Cook for 1-2 mins or brown under a hot grill before serving.

FISH AND BUTTER BEAN CASSEROLE *Serves 4*
Cooking time: about 16 mins

25g (1 oz) butter
1 bunch of spring onions, chopped
30ml (2 tbsp) flour
150ml (¼ pt) vegetable or fish stock
300ml (½ pt) milk
60ml (4 tbsp) dry white wine
30ml (2 tbsp) chopped fresh parsley
450g (1 lb) white fish, such as cod, haddock, whiting
**   or plaice, skinned and boned**
450g (1 lb) smoked fish, such as haddock or cod,
**   skinned and boned**
415g can butter beans, drained
salt and freshly ground black pepper

1. Put the butter and onions in a large casserole, cover and cook for 2 mins.

2. Stir in the flour then gradually stir in the stock and milk. Cook for 5 mins, stirring frequently, until boiling.

3. Add the wine and parsley. Cut the fish into chunks and add to the casserole. Stir in the butter beans and season to taste.

4. Cover and cook for 10 mins, stirring gently once or twice, until the fish is cooked. Serve immediately.

SALMON WITH CREAMY CHIVE SAUCE

Cooking time: about 10 mins   *Serves 2*

2 salmon cutlets or fillets
150ml (¼ pt) vegetable stock
100ml (4 fl oz) dry white vermouth
15ml (1 tbsp) lemon juice
30ml (2 tbsp) chopped chives
75ml (5 tbsp) double cream
salt and freshly ground black pepper

1. Put the salmon in a shallow dish and add the stock and vermouth. Cover and cook for 4 mins or until the fish is just cooked.

2. Lift the salmon on to a serving plate and keep warm.

3. Cook the remaining liquid, uncovered, for about 5 mins or until reduced by half. Stir in the lemon juice, chives and cream. Season to taste with salt and pepper, then cook for 30 secs.

4. Serve the sauce with the salmon.

SALMON WITH CUCUMBER SAUCE   *Serves 1*
Cooking time: about 6 mins

knob of butter
40g (1¹/₂ oz) cucumber, skin left on and cut into small strips
2.5ml (¹/₂ tsp) dried tarragon, or 5ml (1 tsp) chopped fresh
salt and freshly ground black pepper
175g (6 oz) salmon steak
1 spring onion, sliced
5ml (1 tsp) cornflour
5ml (1 tsp) white wine vinegar or lemon juice
15ml (1 tbsp) double cream

1. Put the butter into a small jug or bowl and heat for about 20 secs until melted.

2. Stir in the cucumber, tarragon and seasoning. Cover and cook for 1 min.

3. Put the salmon in a small shallow dish and sprinkle the onion over. Cover and cook for about 2 mins or until just cooked. Cover and leave to stand.

4. Meanwhile, pour the juices from around the fish into the cucumber mixture. Stir in the cornflour and vinegar or lemon juice. Cook, stirring frequently, until the sauce thickens and boils. Stir in the cream.

5. Serve the salmon with the sauce poured over.

PRAWNS A LA PROVENCALE

Serves 4

Cooking time: about 15 mins

10ml (2 tsp) olive oil
1 medium onion, finely chopped
1 garlic clove, crushed
1 green pepper, seeds removed and finely chopped
1 celery stick, finely sliced
30ml (2 tbsp) cornflour
400g can chopped tomatoes
2.5ml (^{1}/$_2$ tsp) sugar
2.5ml (^{1}/$_2$ tsp) dried mixed herbs
salt and freshly ground black pepper
350g (12 oz) cooked shelled prawns, thawed if frozen
cooked rice or pasta, to serve

1. Put the oil, onion, garlic, pepper and celery in a bowl, cover and cook for 5 mins, stirring once or twice.

2. Stir in the cornflour, then add the tomatoes, sugar, herbs and seasonings. Cover and cook for 8 mins, stirring once or twice.

3. Add the prawns and cook for 2 mins, stirring once. Leave to stand for 2-3 mins before serving with rice or pasta.

SWEET AND SOUR PRAWNS

Serves 1

Cooking time: about 12 mins

5ml (1 tsp) cornflour
45ml (3 tbsp) tomato ketchup
10ml (2 tsp) chilli sauce
1 garlic clove, crushed
225g (8 oz) shelled prawns, thawed if frozen
5ml (1 tsp) lemon juice
225g (8 oz) beansprouts
15ml (1 tbsp) soy sauce

1. Put the cornflour into a medium bowl, add 30ml (2 tbsp) water and stir until blended. Add the ketchup, chilli sauce and garlic and mix well. Cook for 2-3 mins, stirring once or twice until the mixture has thickened.

2. Stir in the prawns, cover and cook on MEDIUM-HIGH (75%) for about 7 mins, stirring once or twice. Add the lemon juice, cover and leave to stand.

3. Meanwhile, put the beansprouts in a medium bowl, cover and cook for about 3 mins, stirring once, or until they have just wilted. Drain and toss them with the soy sauce.

4. Serve the beansprouts topped with the prawns and their sauce.

MARINATED PRAWN KEBABS

Serves 4

Cooking time: about 4 mins (plus marinating)

16 large raw prawns, heads removed
45ml (3 tbsp) clear honey
15ml (1 tbsp) lemon juice or white wine vinegar
30ml (2 tbsp) light soy sauce
30ml (2 tbsp) tomato ketchup
green salad and lemon wedges, to serve

1. Thread the prawns on to four bamboo skewers, leaving a small gap between each prawn. Lay them in a shallow dish.

2. Mix together the remaining ingredients and pour over the prawns, coating them well. Cover and marinate for about 2 hours, turning the skewers occasionally.

3. Lift the skewers out of the marinade and arrange them on a plate – either around the edge, or like spokes of a wheel.

4. Cook, uncovered, for 3-4 mins, rearranging them half way, or until the prawns are cooked (they will turn pink).

5. Serve with green salad and lemon wedges.

SEAFOOD KEBABS
Serves 1
Cooking time: about 3 mins

**125g (4 oz) firm fish fillet, such as monkfish, halibut
or salmon
2 whole, unpeeled prawns, thawed if frozen
2 lemon or lime wedges
15g (¹/₂ oz) butter
15ml (1 tbsp) chopped fresh tarragon or mint
5ml (1 tsp) finely grated lemon or lime rind
salt and freshly ground black pepper**

1. Cut the fish into cubes. Thread the fish, prawns and lemon or lime wedges on to two wooden kebab sticks.

2. Put the butter in a small bowl and cook for about 30 secs until melted. Stir in the tarragon or mint and the lemon or lime rind. Brush the mixture over the kebabs, coating them well.

3. Put the kebabs on a plate and cook on MEDIUM-HIGH (75%) for 2-3 mins or until the fish is just cooked.

4. Season to taste before serving.

MOULES MARINIERE

Serves 1

Cooking time: about 5 mins

15g (¹/₂ oz) butter
3 spring onions, sliced
0.5 litre (1 pt) fresh mussels
freshly ground black pepper
30-45ml (2-3 tbsp) dry white wine
30ml (2 tbsp) double cream
chopped fresh parsley

1. Put the butter in a large bowl and cook for about 30 secs or until melted.

2. Stir in the onions, cover and cook for 1 min.

3. Add the mussels, pepper and wine, cover and cook for 2-3 mins, shaking once or twice, until all the mussels have opened (discard those that do not).

4. Use a slotted spoon to lift the mussels on to a warmed serving dish.

5. Stir the cream into the juices in the bowl and cook for 30 secs.

6. Pour the sauce over the mussels and generously sprinkle with parsley.

KEDGEREE

Serves 4-6

Cooking time: about 20 mins

2 eggs
450g (1 lb) smoked haddock fillets
225g (8 oz) long grain rice
30ml (2 tbsp) chopped parsley
25g (1 oz) butter
salt and freshly ground pepper

1. Either hard-boil the eggs conventionally (on the hob) or cook them following the method for Baked Eggs on page 155. Leave to cool.

2. Put the haddock in a shallow dish, cover and cook for about 5 mins or until just cooked. Leave to stand for 5 mins.

3. Meanwhile, put the rice into a large bowl and pour over 600ml (1 pt) boiling water. Stir well. Cook uncovered for 10 mins. Cover and leave to stand for 5 mins.

4. Flake the haddock, discarding skin and bones. Shell the eggs, if necessary, and roughly chop them.

5. Gently mix together the rice, haddock, eggs, parsley and butter. Season to taste.

6. Reheat, if necessary, for 2-3 mins before serving.

8
Sauces and Stuffings

Smooth sauces are quick to make in the microwave and can be conveniently cooked in a serving jug or bowl. Even small quantities do not stick or burn, as they often do when cooked in a saucepan on the hob. Most sauces reheat well in the microwave too.

HANDY HINTS – SAUCES

● Use a jug or bowl which is large enough to allow the sauce to boil up.

● Cover most sauces during cooking, unless you are cooking a very small quantity and a cover would be a nuisance when stirring frequently. Sauces which contain milk easily boil over if covered, so it's more convenient to cook them uncovered.

● Most sauces can be cooked on HIGH (100%), but those containing eggs are best cooked on MEDIUM (50%) or MEDIUM-LOW (30%) to prevent curdling.

● Stir or whisk sauces frequently during cooking to prevent lumps forming.

● To develop the flavour of a cooked sauce (such as tomato sauce), or to thicken or reduce it further, continue cooking, uncovered on MEDIUM (50%) or MEDIUM-LOW (30%) until the desired flavour and consistency are achieved.

- Reheat sauces on HIGH (100%), stirring occasionally. Small quantities (150ml/¼ pt or less) may be better on MEDIUM (50%).

- *Frozen sauces* can be reheated straight from the freezer. Put the frozen block in a bowl and cook on HIGH (100%), breaking up the sauce as it thaws. Once it has thawed, stir or whisk the sauce occasionally during reheating.

WHITE SAUCE   *Serves 4-6*
Cooking time: about 7 mins   ✲
Serve with vegetables, fish or ham.

40g (1½ oz) butter
40g (1½ oz) flour
600ml (1 pt) milk
salt and freshly ground pepper

Method 1
1. Put the butter in a large bowl or jug. Cook for 1 min until melted.

2. Stir in the flour, then gradually blend in the milk.

3. Cook, uncovered, for 5-6 mins or until the sauce thickens and boils, whisking frequently. Season to taste.

Method 2
1. Put the milk in a large bowl or jug. Cut the butter into small pieces and add to the milk. Cook for 1-2 mins to melt the butter. Stir well.

2. Whisk in the flour until smooth.

3. Cook for 5-6 mins or until the sauce thickens and boils, whisking frequently. Season to taste.

CHEESE SAUCE

Follow the method for WHITE SAUCE and add 75-100g (3-4 oz) grated cheese to the cooked sauce. Stir until melted.

MUSHROOM SAUCE

Follow Method 1 for WHITE SAUCE. At stage 1, add 100g (4 oz) finely sliced or chopped mushrooms to the butter, cover and cook for 2 mins.

MUSTARD SAUCE

Follow the method for WHITE SAUCE. Add 30ml (2 tbsp) ready-made mustard to the cooked sauce.

ONION SAUCE

Follow Method 1 for WHITE SAUCE. At stage 1, add a finely chopped onion to the butter, cover and cook for 3 mins.

PARSLEY SAUCE

Follow the method for WHITE SAUCE and add 30-45ml (2-3 tbsp) parsley to the cooked sauce.

PRAWN SAUCE

Follow the method for WHITE SAUCE. Add 100g (4 oz) small peeled prawns and 15ml (1 tbsp) lemon juice to the cooked sauce. Cook for 1 min.

BREAD SAUCE

Serves 4-6

Cooking time: about 20 mins

❄

Serve with turkey or chicken.

1 small onion, finely sliced
1 bay leaf
6 black peppercorns
2 cloves
pinch of ground nutmeg
300ml (½ pt) milk
50g (2 oz) fresh white breadcrumbs
salt and freshly ground pepper
25g (1 oz) butter

1. Put the onion, bay leaf, peppercorns, cloves, nutmeg and milk into a large bowl or jug. Cook, uncovered, on HIGH (100%) for 3-5 mins or until it just begins to boil.

2. Cover and continue cooking on MEDIUM-LOW (30%) for 10 mins.

3. Strain, discarding the onion, bay leaf, peppercorns and cloves. Return the milk to the bowl or jug. Stir in the breadcrumbs, season to taste and add the butter.

4. Cover and cook on MEDIUM (50%) for 5 mins, stirring occasionally, until the sauce is thick.

APPLE SAUCE

Cooking time: about 5 mins

Serves 4

❄

Serve with roast pork, duck or goose.

225g (8 oz) cooking apples, peeled, cored and sliced
10ml (2 tbsp) caster sugar (optional)
small knob of butter

1. Put the apples in a bowl with 15ml (1 tbsp) water and the sugar if using. Cover and cook for 5 mins, stirring occasionally, or until the apples are soft and partially puréed.

2. Stir in the butter and serve hot or cold.

CRANBERRY SAUCE

Cooking time: about 15 mins

Serves 6

Serve with turkey, duck, game or lamb.

225g (8 oz) cranberries
granulated sugar

1. Put the cranberries into a large bowl and add 300ml (½ pt) water.

2. Cook on HIGH (100%) for about 3 mins or until boiling, then continue cooking on MEDIUM (50%) for about 5 minutes or until the cranberries pop open.

3. Add sugar to taste and stir until dissolved.

4. Cook on MEDIUM (50%) for about 7 mins, stirring occasionally, to reduce and thicken the sauce.

5. Serve hot or cold.

HOLLANDAISE SAUCE

Serves 4

Cooking time: about 2 mins

Serve with fish (salmon is a favourite) or vegetables (asparagus is traditional). Use really fresh eggs for this sauce. Since the egg yolks cook only to a thickened (and not fully cooked) stage, this recipe is not recommended for those at risk from salmonella.

100g (4 oz) butter
30ml (2 tbsp) white wine vinegar
2 egg yolks
salt and freshly ground pepper

1. Cut the butter into small pieces and put into a bowl. Cook for $\frac{1}{2}$-1 min until just melted (stir to help it melt if necessary – the butter must not get too hot).

2. Add the vinegar, egg yolks and a little seasoning. Whisk well.

3. Cook on MEDIUM (50%), whisking after every 15 secs, until the sauce just thickens. Take care not to overcook or the sauce will curdle.

STILTON SAUCE
Cooking time: about 5 mins

Serves 2

Serve with grilled steak or vegetables.

15g (¹/₂ oz) butter
1 small onion, finely chopped
30ml (2 tbsp) dry sherry
100ml (4 fl oz) crème fraîche
50g (2 oz) Blue Stilton cheese
15ml (1 tbsp) snipped chives

1. Put the butter and onion in a bowl, cover and cook for 3 mins.

2. Stir in the sherry and cream and cook for 1-2 mins, stirring once.

3. Crumble in the cheese and stir until melted and the sauce is smooth.

4. Stir in the chives and serve immediately.

97

CREAMY CURRY SAUCE

Cooking time: about 17 mins

Serves 4-6

❀

Serve with hard-boiled eggs, vegetables, fish, meat or poultry.

15ml (1 tbsp) oil
1 large onion, finely chopped
1 garlic clove, crushed
1 large eating apple, peeled, cored and chopped
15ml (1 tbsp) flour
300ml (¹/₂ pt) vegetable or chicken stock
30ml (2 tbsp) curry paste
15ml (1 tbsp) tomato purée
50g (2 oz) creamed coconut, chopped
15ml (1 tbsp) lemon juice
salt and freshly ground black pepper
150ml (¹/₄ pt) single cream

1. Put the oil, onion and garlic into a bowl or jug, cover and cook for 3 mins.

2. Add the apple and then stir in the flour. Blend in the stock, curry paste, tomato purée and coconut.

3. Cook for 3 mins or until the sauce boils, then cook on MEDIUM (50%) for about 10 mins, stirring occasionally.

4. Stir in the lemon juice and season with salt and pepper. Add the cream and cook for 1 min.

BOLOGNESE SAUCE

Serves 4

Cooking time: about 30 mins ❄

Serve with pasta or as a filling for jacket potatoes (page 164).

15ml (1 tbsp) oil
1 large onion, finely chopped
1 garlic clove, crushed
100g (4 oz) lean streaky bacon, rinds removed and finely chopped
2 medium carrots, finely chopped
450g (1 lb) lean minced beef
150ml (¼ pt) beef stock
30ml (2 tbsp) tomato purée
2.5ml (½ tsp) dried mixed herbs
2.5ml (½ tsp) dried oregano
salt and freshly ground black pepper

1. Put the oil, onion, garlic, bacon and carrots in a large bowl. Cover and cook for 5 mins, stirring once.

2. Break up the minced beef and add to the bowl. Cover and cook for 5 mins, stirring once.

3. Add the remaining ingredients and stir well. Cover and cook for 15-20 mins, stirring occasionally.

CHILLI SAUCE

Follow the recipe for BOLOGNESE SAUCE, adding a drained 400g can red kidney beans in step 3, and chilli powder to taste.

BARBECUE SAUCE

Serves 4-6

Cooking time: about 15 mins ❄

Serve with burgers, steaks, poultry or vegetables.

15ml (1 tbsp) oil
1 large onion, finely chopped
300ml ($^1/_2$ pt) vegetable stock
45ml (3 tbsp) red wine vinegar
45ml (3 tbsp) brown sugar
45ml (3 tbsp) tomato purée
45ml (3 tbsp) Worcestershire sauce
15ml (1 tbsp) ready-made mustard
5ml (1 tsp) dried mixed herbs
salt and freshly ground black pepper

1. Put the oil and onion in a bowl, cover and cook for 5 mins.

2. Stir in the remaining ingredients, cover and cook for about 8 mins, stirring once or twice. For a thicker sauce, uncover and continue cooking, stirring occasionally, until the sauce has reduced and thickened.

TOMATO SAUCE

Serves 4-6

Cooking time: about 13 mins

❄

Serve with pasta, vegetables, fish, meat or poultry.

10ml (2 tsp) oil
1 small onion, finely chopped
1 small carrot, finely chopped
1 garlic clove, crushed
15ml (1 tbsp) cornflour
400g can chopped tomatoes or 450g (1 lb) fresh ripe
**   tomatoes, skinned and chopped**
300ml (¹/₂ pt) chicken or vegetable stock
15ml (1 tbsp) sugar
15ml (1 tbsp) tomato purée
salt and freshly ground black pepper

1. Put the oil, onion, carrot and garlic in a bowl or jug, cover and cook for 3 mins.

2. Stir in the cornflour, then add the remaining ingredients.

3. Cover and cook for about 10 mins, stirring occasionally.

SWEET WHITE SAUCE

Serves 4

Cooking time: about 4 mins

❄

Serve with sponge and fruit puddings.

15g (¹/₂ oz) cornflour
300ml (¹/₂ pt) milk
knob of butter
15ml (1 tbsp) caster sugar
few drops of vanilla essence

1. In a bowl or jug, mix the cornflour to a smooth paste with a little of the milk.

2. Heat the remaining milk for 2 mins. Pour on to the cornflour mixture and whisk well.

3. Cook for 2 mins, whisking frequently, until the sauce thickens and boils.

4. Stir in butter, sugar and vanilla essence.

BRANDY SAUCE

Follow method for SWEET WHITE SAUCE. At stage 4, add 30ml (2 tbsp) brandy.

CHOCOLATE SAUCE

Serves 4-6

Cooking time: about 3 mins   ❋

Serve with ice cream, chocolate sponge pudding, bananas or poached pears.

175g (6 oz) plain chocolate
45ml (3 tbsp) golden syrup
25g (1 oz) butter
15ml (1 tbsp) lemon juice

1. Break the chocolate into a bowl. Add the remaining ingredients plus 30ml (2 tbsp) water.

2. Cook, uncovered, on MEDIUM (50%) for about 3 mins, stirring occasionally, until melted, smooth and glossy.

JAM SAUCE

Serves 4

Cooking time: about 4 mins   ❋

Serve hot with sponge puddings; hot or cold with ice cream.

60ml (4 tbsp) jam
10ml (2 tsp) cornflour

1. Put the jam in a bowl or jug and add 150ml ($^1/_4$ pt) water. Cook for 2 mins and stir well until the jam melts.

2. Mix the cornflour to a smooth paste with a little water. Stir into the jam mixture.

3. Cook for 2 mins, stirring frequently, until the sauce thickens and boils.

SUMMER FRUIT SAUCE

Serves 6

Cooking time: about 8 mins ❄

Serve with ice cream, poached fruit, meringues or sponge puddings.

225g (8 oz) frozen summer fruit
175g (6 oz) redcurrant jelly
50ml (2 fl oz) port
10ml (2 tsp) cornflour

1. Put the fruit in a bowl and cook for about 3 mins, stirring once, until thawed.

2. Add the jelly and port. Cook for 4 mins, stirring frequently, or until the jelly has melted.

3. Mix the cornflour to a smooth paste with a little water. Add a little of the warm fruit then stir the mixture into the bowl.

4. Cook for 1 min or until the sauce thickens and boils.

BUTTERSCOTCH SAUCE

Serves 4

Cooking time: about 4 mins ❄

Serve with ice cream, bananas or sponge puddings.

50g (2 oz) butter
50g (2 oz) brown sugar
175g (6 oz) golden syrup
10ml (2 tsp) lemon juice
150ml (¹/₄ pt) double cream

1. Put the butter, sugar and syrup into a bowl or jug and cook for 2-3 mins until melted.

2. Stir until well blended.

3. Stir in the lemon juice and cream. Heat for ¹/₂-1 min before serving.

SAGE AND ONION STUFFING

Serves 4-6

Cooking time: about 5 mins ❄

Serve with pork or duck.

225g (8 oz) onions, finely chopped
25g (1 oz) butter
100g (4 oz) fresh breadcrumbs
5ml (1 tsp) dried sage
salt and freshly ground black pepper
milk

1. Put the onions and butter into a medium bowl, cover and cook for 5 mins, stirring once.

2. Stir in the breadcrumbs, sage and seasoning, binding it all together with a little milk if necessary.

3. Use as required.

CHESTNUT STUFFING

Serves 4-6

Cooking time: about 15 mins ❄

Serve with chicken or turkey.

100g (4 oz) dried chestnuts, soaked overnight
40g (1$^{1}/_{2}$ oz) butter
100g (4 oz) fresh breadcrumbs
10ml (2 tsp) finely grated onion
1.25ml ($^{1}/_{4}$ tsp) ground nutmeg
30ml (2 tbsp) chopped fresh parsley
salt and freshly ground black pepper
milk

1. Drain the chestnuts, discarding their soaking water. Put them into a medium bowl and pour over sufficient boiling water to just cover them. Cover and cook for 10-15 mins until just tender. Leave to stand for 5 mins.

2. Drain and finely chop the chestnuts.

3. Heat the butter for 45 secs or until melted. Stir in the chestnuts and the remaining ingredients, binding them together with a little milk if necessary.

4. Use as required.

PARSLEY AND LEMON STUFFING *Serves 4-6*
Cooking time: about 5 mins ❈

Serve with chicken, turkey, lamb or fish.

225g (8 oz) onions, finely chopped
25g (1 oz) butter
100g (4 oz) fresh breadcrumbs
45ml (3 tbsp) chopped fresh parsley
grated rind and juice of ½ a lemon
1 small egg, lightly beaten
salt and freshly ground black pepper

1. Put the onions and butter in a medium bowl, cover and cook for 5 mins, stirring once.

2. Stir in the remaining ingredients and use as required.

WALNUT AND ORANGE STUFFING *Serves 4-6*
Cooking time: about 5 mins ❈

Serve with chicken, turkey or goose.

225g (8 oz) onions, finely chopped
25g (1 oz) butter
100g (4 oz) fresh breadcrumbs
15ml (1 tbsp) chopped fresh parsley
25g (1 oz) finely chopped walnuts
1 large orange
salt and freshly ground black pepper

1. Put the onions and butter into a medium bowl, cover and cook for 5 mins, stirring once.

2. Stir in the breadcrumbs, parsley and walnuts.

3. Grate the rind from the orange and add to the mixture. Squeeze the juice from half the orange, add to the stuffing and mix well. Season with salt and pepper.

4. Use as required.

9

Meat and Poultry

Meat and poultry can be thawed and cooked in the microwave. It is particularly suitable for bacon rashers and joints; whole poultry and poultry pieces; minced meat; and cubes of beef, pork, lamb, bacon and poultry for cooking in a sauce. Whether you cook joints of meat, chops and steaks will depend on personal taste, unless you have a combination cooker (which browns and crisps as well as cooking quickly with microwaves). Here, you will find plenty of tips on how to get the best results.

HANDY HINTS – THAWING MEAT AND POULTRY

● Remove any metal tags from the wrappings.

● Stand the meat or poultry on a microwave or roasting rack – to lift it above the liquid which collects beneath.

● Thaw on DEFROST or MEDIUM-LOW (30%).

- Separate items like bacon rashers, chops and steaks as they begin to thaw. Reposition them occasionally too.

- Turn large pieces, joints and whole birds over at least once during thawing.

- Pour away any moisture as it collects around the meat or poultry during thawing. If you don't, the liquid will heat up while the rest remains frozen.

- If any parts begin to warm up, stop thawing and leave the meat or poultry to stand for about 20 mins before continuing.

- When thawing is completed, leave small pieces to stand for at least 10 mins before cooking. Large pieces, whole poultry and joints need at least 30 mins.

Guide to thawing times	
Per 450g (1 lb) on DEFROST or MEDIUM-LOW (30%)	
Beef joints, on bone	10-12 mins
boneless	8-10 mins
Beef, steak	8-10 mins
Lamb joints	5-6 mins
Pork/bacon joints	7-8 mins
Chops	8-10 mins
Cubed & minced meat	7-10 mins
Liver & kidney	7-9 mins
Chicken, whole	6-8 mins
Turkey, whole	10-12 mins
Chicken & turkey portions	5-7 mins

HANDY HINTS – COOKING MEAT AND POULTRY

- Thaw meat and poultry completely before cooking (see page 107).

- Regular shapes, such as boned and rolled joints, cook more evenly than irregular shapes, such as a leg joint.

- Meat on the bone tends to cook more quickly than off the bone.

- Secure large items with string or with wooden (not metal) skewers.

- Season with salt after cooking, to prevent the surface from drying and shrinking. Only if the meat or poultry is immersed in liquid can a little salt be added during cooking.

- Put large pieces and joints on a microwave or roasting rack, so they do not sit in their juices during cooking.

- A browning dish can be useful for cooking chops and sausages (follow the dish manufacturer's instructions).

- Arrange small pieces, like chicken drumsticks, with their thinner ends towards the centre of the dish.

- Arrange small even-shaped pieces, such as meatballs, around the edge of the dish.

- Meat loaves cook best in a ring-shaped mould.

- Cover during cooking to keep moisture in, to help the meat or poultry to cook evenly, and to keep the oven walls free from splashes.

- Cover joints or whole poultry with a split microwave or roasting bag, to encourage a little browning of the surface.

- Joints and whole poultry are usually cooked on HIGH (100%)-see ** in the cooking guide on page 111. Check with your microwave manufacturer's instructions too. Meat and poultry which is immersed in liquid can be brought to the boil on HIGH (100%), then cooked on MEDIUM (50%) or MEDIUM-LOW (30%) until the meat or poultry is tender – just like boiling and simmering on the hob.

- Turn large pieces, whole poultry and joints at least once during cooking.

- Stir casserole-style dishes occasionally during cooking.

- The cooking time for meat will depend on the cut. "Braising" and "stewing" cuts will need long, slow cooking in order to tenderize them – just as they would on the hob or in the conventional oven. Their cooking time will still be reduced by about one third in the microwave.

- Check that meat and poultry is cooked by inserting a skewer into the thickest part. The juices should always run clear from pork and poultry, though you may prefer them pink in beef and lamb. If you use a meat thermometer, insert it into the thickest part of the meat and make sure it does not touch any bone.

- A meat thermometer should not be left in the meat during cooking unless it is specially designed for the microwave.

- Leave joints and whole poultry to stand for 15-20 mins after cooking – to allow the temperature to even out to make carving easier.

Guide to cooking times	
Per 450g (1 lb) on HIGH (100%)	
Beef, rare	5-6 mins
medium	6-7 mins
well done	8-9 mins
Lamb, medium	7-8 mins
well done	8-10 mins
Pork	8-10 mins
Bacon	9-12 mins
Liver & kidney	6-8 mins
Chicken, whole	8-10 mins
Turkey, whole	9-11 mins
Chicken & turkey portions	6-8 mins

** If you find that meat and poultry cooked on HIGH (100%) overcooks, try cooking on HIGH (100%) for the first few minutes, then reducing the power to MEDIUM-HIGH (75%) or MEDIUM (50%) until cooked through.

	on HIGH (100%)
Chops, 1	2-4 mins
2	3-5 mins
3	4-6 mins
4	5-7 mins
Bacon rasher, 2	2-3 mins
4	4-5 mins
6	5-6 mins
Chicken breast, boneless	2-3 mins

BEEF IN STOUT

Serves 4

Cooking time: about 1½-1¾ hrs ❄

2 lean streaky bacon rashers, rinds removed and chopped
225g (8 oz) leeks, thinly sliced
2 celery sticks, thinly sliced
25g (1 oz) flour
salt and freshly ground black pepper
700g (1½ lb) lean braising beef, cut into cubes
2 beef stock cubes
300ml (½ pt) stout
175g (6 oz) no-soak ready-to-eat prunes, stoned
30ml (2 tbsp) tomato purée
5ml (1 tsp) dried mixed herbs

1. Put the bacon, leeks and celery in a large casserole, cover and cook for 5 mins, stirring once.

2. Meanwhile, season the flour with salt and pepper and toss the beef in it until well coated. Stir the beef and any excess flour into the vegetables.

3. Dissolve the stock cubes in 60ml (4 tbsp) boiling water and add to the casserole with the remaining ingredients. Stir well.

4. Cover and cook on HIGH (100%) for 10 mins or until boiling. Continue cooking on MEDIUM-LOW (30%) for 1¼-1½ hrs, stirring occasionally, until the beef is tender.

BEEF IN RED WINE

Serves 4

Cooking time: about 1¹/₄ hrs   ❄

1 medium onion, chopped
1 large garlic clove, crushed
100g (4 oz) lean streaky bacon, rinds removed and
   chopped
10ml (2 tsp) oil
30ml (2 tbsp) flour
salt and freshly ground black pepper
700g (1¹/₂ lb) lean braising beef, cut into cubes
1 bouquet garni
300ml (¹/₂ pt) red wine
100g (4 oz) button mushrooms

1. Put the onion, garlic, bacon and oil into a large casserole. Cover and cook for 5 mins, stirring once.

2. Meanwhile put the flour into a polythene food bag and season with salt and pepper. Add the beef and shake well to coat it with the seasoned flour. Tip the beef and any excess flour into the onion mixture and stir well. Add the bouquet garni and wine.

3. Cover and cook on HIGH (100%) for 10 mins or until boiling. Stir, then continue to cook on MEDIUM (50%) for 1-1¹/₂ hrs or until the beef is tender, stirring occasionally.

4. Stir in the mushrooms and cook for 3 mins.

BEEF AND VEGETABLE CASSEROLE   *Serves 4*

Cooking time: 1¹/₄-1³/₄ hrs   ❊

10ml (2 tsp) oil
1 medium onion, sliced
2 celery sticks, sliced
225g (8 oz) carrots, sliced
225g (8 oz) parsnip, swede or turnip, chopped
450g (1 lb) lean braising beef, cut into cubes
30ml (2 tbsp) flour
300ml (¹/₂ pt) beef stock
15ml (1 tbsp) dried mixed herbs
10ml (2 tsp) mustard powder
30ml (2 tbsp) tomato purée
salt and freshly ground black pepper

1. Put the oil and vegetables into a large casserole, cover and cook for 5 mins, stirring once.

2. Add the beef, cover and cook for 5 mins, stirring once.

3. Stir in the flour, then add the remaining ingredients and mix well.

4. Cover and cook on HIGH (100%) for 5 mins. Continue cooking, covered, on MEDIUM-LOW (30%) for 1-1¹/₂ hrs, stirring occasionally, until the beef is tender.

COTTAGE PIE

Cooking time: about 18 mins
(plus Bolognese Sauce and grilling)

✳

1 quantity Bolognese Sauce (page 99)
550g (1¹/₄ lb) potatoes, sliced
salt and freshly ground pepper
butter
milk

1. Spoon the meat sauce into a flameproof dish.

2. Put the potatoes into a large bowl with 60ml (4 tbsp) water. Cover and cook for about 8 mins until the potatoes are tender, stirring occasionally. Mash the potatoes with seasoning, butter and milk to taste.

3. Spoon the potatoes on top of the meat mixture.

4. Reheat, uncovered, on MEDIUM (50%) for about 10 mins, and brown under a hot grill if wished.

BEEF WITH GINGER AND SPRING ONIONS

Serves 2

Cooking time: about 6 mins (plus marinating)

350g (12 oz) fillet steak
15ml (1 tbsp) finely grated fresh root ginger
1 garlic clove, crushed
60ml (4 tbsp) dry sherry
60ml (4 tbsp) light soy sauce
5ml (1 tsp) clear honey
10ml (2 tsp) oil
20ml (4 tsp) cornflour
1 bunch of spring onions, thickly sliced
cooked rice, to serve

1. Cut the steaks into thin strips across the grain and put into a bowl. Mix together the ginger, garlic, sherry, soy sauce and honey. Pour the mixture over the steak, stirring to coat it well. Cover and marinate in a cool place for 1 hour or more.

2. Put the oil into a large bowl. Use a slotted spoon to lift the steak out of its marinade and stir the steak into the oil. Cook, uncovered for 2 mins, or until the steak is just cooked, stirring once.

3. Whisk the cornflour into the marinade and pour over the steak.

4. Add the onions and cook, uncovered, for 3-4 mins, stirring frequently, until the sauce thickens and boils.

5. Serve with hot rice.

BEEF WITH LAYERED POTATOES

Serves 4

Cooking time: about 45 mins (plus grilling)   ❊

10ml (2 tsp) oil
2 medium onions, finely chopped
450g (1 lb) lean minced beef
1 beef stock cube
198g can sweetcorn with peppers
15ml (1 tbsp) dried mixed herbs
30ml (2 tbsp) tomato purée
10ml (2 tsp) flour
salt and freshly ground black pepper
550g (1¼ lb) potatoes, thinly sliced
25g (1 oz) butter

1. Put the oil and onions in a large bowl, cover and cook for 5 mins, stirring once.

2. Break up the beef and stir into the onions. Add the crumbled stock cube, sweetcorn with peppers, herbs, tomato purée, flour and seasoning. Stir well.

3. Cover and cook for 10 mins, stirring twice.

4. Spoon the beef mixture into a flameproof dish. Arrange the potatoes on top, seasoning the layers lightly with salt and pepper.

5. Put the butter in a small bowl, cook for 30 secs or until melted and brush it over the top of the potatoes.

6. Cover and cook on MEDIUM (50%) for 20-30 mins until the potatoes are cooked through (they should yield easily to a skewer or knife).

7. Before serving, brown under a hot grill until the top is crisp.

MEAT LOAF RING

Cooking time: about 20 mins

Serves 6
❄

700g (1¹/₂ lb) lean minced beef
100g (4 oz) fresh breadcrumbs
1 medium onion, finely chopped
1-2 beef stock cubes
30ml (2 tbsp) tomato purée
15ml (1 tbsp) French mustard
5ml (1 tsp) dried mixed herbs
salt and freshly ground black pepper
2 eggs, beaten
4 bay leaves
4 green olives stuffed with pimento, sliced

1. Put all the ingredients, except the bay leaves and olives, into a large bowl and thoroughly mix.

2. Lightly grease a 23cm (9 in) diameter ring mould. Line its base with microwave or non-stick paper.

3. Arrange the bay leaves and olive slices on the paper. Carefully spoon the meat mixture on top, pressing it down into the mould and levelling the top.

4. Cover and cook on MEDIUM (50%) for about 20 mins or until cooked through.

5. Leave to stand, covered, for 10 mins before turning out and serving hot or cold.

MEATBALLS IN SPICY SAUCE

Cooking time: about 15-20 mins

450g (1 lb) lean minced beef
1 small onion, finely chopped
15ml (1 tbsp) dried mixed herbs
1 egg, beaten
150ml (¼ pt) beef stock
15ml (1 tbsp) horseradish sauce
15ml (1 tbsp) Worcestershire sauce
15ml (1 tbsp) tomato purée
10ml (2 tsp) cornflour
few drops of hot chilli sauce
salt and freshly ground black pepper

1. Mix together the beef, onion, herbs and egg and shape into 16 balls. Arrange them in a large shallow dish and cook, uncovered for about 5 mins, rearranging them half way through cooking.

2. Whisk together the remaining ingredients and pour over and around the meatballs. Cover and cook on MEDIUM (50%) for 10-15 mins, stirring gently occasionally until the meatballs are cooked.

BEEF KEBABS WITH HERBS

Serves 1

Cooking time: about 5 mins

100g (4 oz) lean minced beef
3-4 spring onions, thinly sliced
pinch of garlic granules
15g (½ oz) fresh breadcrumbs
10ml (2 tsp) tomato purée
salt and freshly ground black pepper
5ml (1 tsp) dried mixed herbs

1. Put all the ingredients in a bowl and mix until well combined. Divide the mixture into three portions.

2. Using your hands, shape the portions into three "sausages" around a wooden kebab stick, squeezing each one firmly so that it stays in place, and leaving a small gap between them.

3. Put the kebab on a microwave rack on a large plate. Cook on MEDIUM-HIGH (75%) for about 5 mins or until cooked, turning the kebab over once.

LAMB CURRY

Serves 4

Cooking time: about 35 mins   ✳

1 medium onion, sliced
2 garlic cloves, crushed
30ml (2 tbsp) curry powder
700g (1¹/₂ lb) lamb fillet or leg, cut into cubes
400g can chopped tomatoes
1 lamb or beef stock cube
salt and freshly ground black pepper
cooked rice, poppadums (see page 251) and mango
    chutney, to serve

1. Put the onion and garlic in a large bowl, cover and cook for 3 mins.

2. Meanwhile, sprinkle the curry powder over the lamb and toss to coat the cubes well.

3. Stir the lamb into the onion. Add the tomatoes and crumble in the stock cube.

4. Cover and cook for 7 mins or until boiling, stirring once or twice. Continue cooking on MEDIUM (50%) for about 25 mins, stirring occasionally, until the lamb is tender. Half way through cooking, season to taste and remove the lid so that the sauce reduces and thickens.

SPICED LAMB WITH MINTED SAUCE *Serves 4*

Cooking time: about 35 mins   ❊

1 medium onion, thinly sliced
2.5ml (½ tsp) ground coriander
2.5ml (½ tsp) ground cumin
450g (1 lb) lamb fillet or leg, thinly sliced
350g (12 oz) button mushrooms
15ml (1 tbsp) flour
150ml (¼ pt) lamb or chicken stock
30ml (2 tbsp) white wine vinegar
45ml (3 tbsp) mint jelly
natural yoghurt, to serve

1. Put the onion in a large bowl, cover and cook for 3 mins.

2. Meanwhile, sprinkle the spices over the lamb and toss to coat the slices well.

3. Add the lamb to the onion and stir in the mushrooms. Cover and cook for 5 mins, stirring once or twice.

4. Stir in the flour, then gradually add the stock. Add the vinegar and the mint jelly.

5. Cook on HIGH (100%) for 5 mins, stirring once or twice, or until boiling. Cover and continue cooking on MEDIUM (50%) for 20-25 mins, stirring occasionally, until the lamb is tender.

6. Serve, topped with a spoonful or two of yoghurt.

HONEYED LAMB WITH ROSEMARY

Serves 1

Cooking time: about 4 mins

1 lean lamb chop, weighing about 175g (6 oz)
1 small garlic clove, thinly sliced
5ml (1 tsp) clear honey
5ml (1 tsp) soy sauce
1 sprig of fresh rosemary, or 2.5ml ($^1/_2$ tsp) dried
freshly ground black pepper

1. Use a sharp knife to make a few slits in the lamb and insert the garlic slices into the slits. Put the chop in a small shallow dish.

2. Mix together the honey and the soy sauce and brush the mixture over the lamb, coating it well. Lay (or sprinkle) the rosemary on top and season with pepper.

3. Cover and cook on MEDIUM-HIGH (75%) for about 5-6 mins or until the lamb is tender.

4. Leave to stand for a few minutes before serving.

MOUSSAKA

Serves 4

Cooking time: about 40 mins
(plus tomato and white sauces, and grilling)

2 medium aubergines
salt
1 quantity Tomato Sauce (page 101)
350g (12 oz) lean minced lamb
50g (2 oz) grated Cheddar cheese
1 egg, lightly beaten
White Sauce, made with 450ml ($^3/_4$ pt) milk (page 92)

1. Thinly slice the aubergines and lightly sprinkle them with salt. Leave to stand in a colander for 10-15 mins. Rinse, drain and dry them.

2. Meanwhile, put the Tomato Sauce into a medium casserole and crumble in the lamb. Stir well, cover and cook for about 8 mins, stirring once or twice.

3. Stir the cheese and egg into the White Sauce.

4. Layer the meat sauce and aubergines in a flameproof dish and top with the cheese sauce.

5. Cover and cook on MEDIUM (50%) for about 30 mins.

6. Brown under a hot grill.

LAMB GOULASH

Cooking time: about 45 mins

Serves 4

❄

700g (1¹/₂ lb) lean lamb leg or fillet, cut into cubes
15ml (1 tbsp) olive oil
1 medium onion, finely chopped
30ml (2 tbsp) flour
400g can tomatoes
2 bay leaves
150ml (¹/₄ pt) red wine or stock
10ml (2 tsp) paprika
salt and freshly ground black pepper
60ml (4 tbsp) natural yoghurt

1. Put the lamb, oil and onion into a large casserole, cover and cook for 5 mins, stirring once.

2. Stir in the flour, then add the remaining ingredients except the yoghurt, mixing well.

3. Cover and cook on HIGH (100%) for 10 mins or until boiling. Stir, cover and continue cooking on MEDIUM (50%) for about 30 mins or until the lamb is tender, stirring occasionally.

4. Spoon the yoghurt on top to serve.

MEDITERRANEAN LAMB

Serves 4

Cooking time: about 35 mins   ✳

10ml (2 tsp) olive oil
1 medium onion, thinly sliced
15ml (1 tbsp) sugar
1 large aubergine, cut into cubes
100g (4 oz) button mushrooms, thickly sliced
1 red pepper, seeds removed and sliced
450g (1 lb) lamb fillet or leg, thinly sliced
150ml (¼ pt) lamb stock
150ml (¼ pt) red wine
30ml (2 tbsp) tomato purée
5ml (1 tsp) dried oregano
salt and freshly ground pepper
cooked rice or pasta, to serve

1. Put the oil, onion and sugar in a large bowl, cover and cook for 3 mins.

2. Add the aubergine, mushrooms and pepper. Cover and cook for 3 mins.

3. Stir in the lamb, then add the stock, wine, tomato purée, oregano and seasoning.

4. Cover and cook on HIGH (100%) for about 8 mins, stirring once or twice, or until boiling. Continue cooking, covered, on MEDIUM (50%) for about 20 mins, stirring occasionally, until the lamb is tender.

5. Serve with hot rice or pasta.

LAMB KORMA

Serves 4

Cooking time: about 28 mins ❄

100g (4 oz) ground almonds
30ml (2 tbsp) mild curry paste
10ml (2 tsp) oil
1 medium onion, finely chopped
700g (1½ lb) lamb fillet or leg, cut into cubes
75ml (3 fl oz) thick natural yoghurt
salt and freshly ground black pepper
75ml (3 fl oz) double cream
lemon wedges, to serve

1. Mix the almonds and curry paste with 150ml (¼ pt) water to make a smooth paste.
2. Put the oil and onion in a large bowl, cover and cook for 3 mins.
3. Add the lamb and stir in the almond mixture and yoghurt. Season with salt and pepper.
4. Cover and cook on HIGH (100%) for 5 mins, stirring once or twice. Continue cooking, covered, on MEDIUM (50%) for about 20 mins, stirring occasionally, until the lamb is tender.
5. Stir in the cream and serve with lemon wedges.

KOFTAS IN CURRY SAUCE

Cooking time: about 28 mins

Serves 4

❋ *without the yoghurt*

450g (1 lb) lean minced lamb
2 garlic cloves, crushed
2 cm (³/₄ inch) fresh root ginger, peeled and grated
1 fresh green chilli, seeds removed and finely chopped
30ml (2 tbsp) chopped fresh coriander or parsley
1 egg, beaten
1 medium onion, finely chopped
5ml (1 tsp) oil
10ml (2 tsp) ground coriander
5ml (1 tsp) ground cumin
2.5ml (¹/₂ tsp) ground turmeric
2.5ml (¹/₂ tsp) ground cinnamon
300ml (¹/₂ pt) lamb or beef stock
30ml (2 tbsp) tomato purée
150ml (¹/₄ pt) natural yoghurt

1. Mix together the lamb, garlic, ginger, chilli, herbs, egg and half the onion. Shape the mixture into 16 small balls (koftas).

2. Arrange the meatballs in a large shallow dish. Cook, uncovered, for about 5 mins, rearranging them once during cooking. Lift them out of the dish and set aside.

3. Put the remaining onion in the dish with the oil. Cover and cook for 3 mins.

4. Stir in the spices, stock and tomato purée. Cover and cook for 5 mins or until boiling.

5. Add the meatballs (with their juices) to the dish and coat them with the sauce. Cook, uncovered, on MEDIUM (50%) for about 15 mins, rearranging the meatballs once during cooking.

6. Stir in the yoghurt before serving.

PORK IN SWEET AND SOUR SAUCE *Serves 4*

Cooking time: about 17 mins ❄

227g can pineapple cubes in fruit juice
chicken or vegetable stock
5ml (1 tsp) oil
1 medium onion, finely sliced
1 garlic clove, crushed
2 celery sticks, finely sliced
450g (1 lb) lean pork, finely sliced
30ml (2 tbsp) tomato purée
45ml (3 tbsp) red wine vinegar
45ml (3 tbsp) soy sauce
45ml (3 tbsp) brown sugar
30ml (2 tbsp) cornflour
salt and freshly ground black pepper
1 green pepper, seeds removed and finely sliced

1. Drain the pineapple and make up the juice to 300ml (½ pt) with chicken or vegetable stock.

2. Put the oil, onion, garlic and celery in a large bowl. Cover and cook for 5 mins, stirring once.

3. Stir in the pork and pineapple-juice mixture.

4. Whisk together the tomato purée, vinegar, soy sauce, sugar and cornflour, then stir into the pork mixture. Season with salt and pepper.

5. Cover and cook for 5 mins, stirring once, or until boiling. Continue cooking, covered, for about 5 mins, stirring twice, or until the pork is tender.

6. Stir in the pepper and pineapple, cover and cook for about 2 mins until hot.

PORK AND BEAN CASSEROLE

Serves 4-6

Cooking time: about 40 mins

❄

15g (¹/₂ oz) butter
5ml (1 tsp) oil
1 large onion, finely sliced
700g (1¹/₂ lb) lean pork, cut into cubes
400g can chopped tomatoes
1 chicken stock cube
15ml (1 tbsp) tomato purée
5ml (1 tsp) dried mixed herbs
salt and freshly ground black pepper
415g can red kidney beans, drained

1. Put the butter, oil and onion in a large bowl, cover and cook for 5 mins, stirring once.

2. Stir in the pork. Add the remaining ingredients and stir well.

3. Cover and cook on HIGH (100%) for about 8 mins, stirring once or twice, or until boiling. Continue cooking, covered, on MEDIUM (50%) for 20-30 mins, stirring occasionally, until the pork is tender.

CHILLI PORK AND BEANS

Cooking time: about 35 mins

Serves 4

✳

1 medium onion, finely chopped
1 garlic clove, crushed
450g (1 lb) pork fillet or tenderloin, thinly sliced
30ml (2 tbsp) flour
5ml (1 tsp) chilli powder
2.5ml (¹/₂ tsp) ground cumin
150ml (¹/₄ pt) chicken, beef or vegetable stock
400g can chopped tomatoes
415g can red kidney beans, drained
salt and freshly ground black pepper

1. Put the onion and garlic in a large bowl, cover and cook for 3 mins.

2. Stir in the pork, cover and cook for 3 mins.

3. Stir in the flour, then add the remaining ingredients and mix well.

4. Cover and cook on HIGH (100%) for about 8 mins, stirring once or twice, or until boiling. Continue cooking on MEDIUM (50%) for about 20 mins, stirring occasionally, until the pork is tender. Remove the cover half way through cooking to help to reduce and thicken the sauce.

PORK ORIENTAL

Serves 4

Cooking time: about 20 mins (plus marinating) ❊

30ml (2 tbsp) soy sauce
15ml (1 tbsp) Worcestershire sauce
60ml (4 tbsp) tomato ketchup
15ml (1 tbsp) brown sugar
15ml (1 tbsp) wholegrain mustard
450g (1 lb) pork fillet or tenderloin, thinly sliced
1 medium onion, thinly sliced
150ml (¼ pt) chicken or vegetable stock
1 red pepper, seeds removed and sliced
100g (4 oz) mushrooms, thickly sliced

1. Mix together the soy sauce, Worcestershire sauce, ketchup, sugar and mustard. Add the pork and stir to coat it well. Cover and leave to marinate in a cool place for 30 mins-2 hrs.

2. Put the onion in a large bowl, cover and cook for 3 mins.

3. Lift the pork out of its marinade and stir the meat into the onion. Cook, uncovered, for 7 mins, stirring once or twice.

4. Add the marinade and stock. Cook, uncovered, for 5 mins, stirring once.

5. Stir in the pepper and mushrooms and cook, uncovered for about 5 mins until the pork is tender, stirring once.

SPARE RIBS BARBECUE-STYLE

Serves 4

Cooking time: about 35 mins (plus marinating) ❋

1 small onion, finely chopped
60ml (4 tbsp) tomato ketchup
60ml (4 tbsp) Worcestershire sauce
15ml (1 tbsp) malt vinegar
10ml (2 tsp) brown sugar
5ml (1 tsp) mustard powder
2.5ml ($^1/_2$ tsp) paprika
900g (2 lb) small lean pork spare ribs

1. To make the marinade, mix together the onion, ketchup, Worcestershire sauce, vinegar, sugar, mustard and paprika. Coat the spare ribs with the mixture and arrange them in a large shallow dish, pouring over any extra marinade. Cover and leave to marinate in a cool place for 1-2 hrs.

2. Cover and cook on HIGH (100%) for 10 mins, then cook on MEDIUM (50%) for a further 10 mins.

3. Rearrange the ribs, then cook uncovered on MEDIUM (50%) for about 15 mins, turning them once or twice, or until they are tender.

HONEYED SPARE RIBS

Serves 1

Cooking time: about 15 mins

350g (12 oz) lean pork spare ribs
2 spring onions, sliced
15ml (1 tbsp) clear honey
5ml (1 tsp) muscovado sugar
few drops of Worcestershire sauce
10ml (2 tsp) tomato ketchup
5ml (1 tsp) French mustard
pinch of ground ginger
pinch of dried mixed herbs
pinch of garlic granules

1. Arrange the ribs in a single layer in a shallow dish. Cover and cook for 3 mins. Drain off and discard any fat.

2. Mix together the remaining ingredients and pour over the ribs, coating them well.

3. Cover and cook for 3 mins then spoon the juices over.

4. Cook, uncovered, on MEDIUM-LOW (30%) for about 5 mins, then spoon the juices over again.

5. Cook, uncovered, on HIGH (100%) for the final 4-5 mins, turning them over once, or until the sauce thickens and coats the ribs well.

6. Leave to stand for a few mins before serving.

BACON AND BUTTER BEAN CASSEROLE

Cooking time: about 30 mins   *Serves 4*

❄

900g (2 lb) lean bacon joint, cut into cubes
1 large onion, sliced
15g (¹/₂ oz) butter
freshly ground black pepper
425g can Cream of Mushroom soup
425g can butter beans, drained

1. Put the bacon into a large bowl, cover with cold water and cook for about 10 mins or until just boiling. Pour off and discard the water.

2. Put the onion and butter into a large casserole, cover and cook for 3 mins.

3. Stir the bacon into the onion and season with pepper. Cover and cook for 10 mins.

4. Stir in the soup and beans, cover and cook on MEDIUM (50%) for about 15 mins or until the bacon is tender, stirring occasionally.

BACON AND APPLE PUDDING

Serves 4

Cooking time: about 15 mins

225g (8 oz) self-raising flour
pinch of salt
100g (4 oz) shredded suet
225g (8 oz) cooked bacon, finely chopped
1 medium onion, finely chopped
50g (2 oz) mushrooms, thinly sliced
1 medium eating apple, peeled, cored and roughly
  grated
5ml (1 tsp) dried sage
150ml ($^1/_4$ pt) chicken stock
freshly ground black pepper

1. Sift the flour and salt into a bowl and stir in the suet.
   Add sufficient cold water to make a soft dough,
   stirring well with a knife. Roll out two-thirds of the
   dough and use it to line a 900ml (1$^1/_2$ pt) pudding
   basin. Roll out the remaining third to make a circle
   large enough for a lid.

2. Mix together all the remaining ingredients and spoon
   into the pastry-lined bowl. Put the pastry lid on top and
   pinch the edges together to seal it securely.

3. Cover with a 'hat' of microwave or non-stick paper
   and cook on MEDIUM-HIGH (75%) for about 15 mins.

4. Leave to stand for 5-10 mins before turning out on to
   a warmed plate and serving.

BACON HOTPOT

Serves 4

Cooking time: about 40 mins (plus grilling)

25g (1 oz) butter
1 medium onion, thinly sliced
225g (8 oz) carrots, thickly sliced
3 celery sticks, chopped
**550g (1¼ lb) lean unsmoked bacon joint, cut into
    cubes**
30ml (2 tbsp) flour
300ml (½ pt) dry cider
15ml (1 tbsp) wholegrain mustard
salt and freshly ground pepper
450g (1 lb) potatoes, thinly sliced

1. Put half the butter in a large flameproof casserole with the onion, carrots and celery. Cover and cook for 5 mins, stirring once.

2. Add the bacon, sprinkle the flour over and stir well. Add the cider, mustard and seasoning.

3. Cover and cook for 10 mins, stirring once or twice, or until boiling.

4. Arrange the potato slices on top, seasoning each layer lightly with salt and pepper. Cover and cook on HIGH (100%) for 5 mins, then continue cooking on MEDIUM-LOW (30%) for about 20 mins or until the bacon and potatoes are tender.

5. Put the remaining butter in a small bowl and cook for 30 secs until melted. Brush the melted butter over the potatoes.

6. Brown under a hot grill until crisp and golden.

AUTUMN BACON CASSEROLE

Serves 4

Cooking time: about 45 mins ❄

15g (½ oz) butter
12 baby onions
450g (1 lb) lean bacon joint, cut into cubes
30ml (1 tbsp) flour
300ml (½ pt) bacon, chicken or vegetable stock
2 medium leeks, sliced
1 large carrot, thinly sliced
400g can tomatoes
50g (2 oz) canned or frozen sweetcorn kernels
freshly ground black pepper

1. Put the butter and onions into a large bowl, cover and cook for 3 mins, stirring once.

2. Add the bacon and stir in the flour. Gradually stir in the stock, add the remaining ingredients and mix well.

3. Cover and cook on HIGH (100%) for about 10 mins, stirring once or twice, or until boiling. Continue cooking, covered, on MEDIUM (50%) for about 30 mins, stirring occasionally, until the bacon is tender.

SOMERSET BACON

Serves 1

Cooking time: about 7 mins

1 medium leek, thinly sliced
1 medium carrot, cut into thin fingers
pinch of dried sage
60ml (4 tbsp) apple juice or dry cider
freshly ground black pepper
1 bacon chop

1. Put the leek, carrot, sage, apple juice and pepper in a bowl. Cover and cook for 3 mins. Stir well.

2. Put the bacon chop on top of the vegetables, cover and cook for 3-4 mins until the bacon has cooked.

3. Leave to stand, covered, for a few mins before serving.

ORANGE-GLAZED GAMMON

Serves 8

Cooking time: about 1 hr (plus grilling)   ✽

1.4kg (3 lb) gammon joint
45ml (3 tbsp) fine-cut orange marmalade
45ml (3 tbsp) demerara sugar

1. Put the gammon in a large casserole and pour over
    sufficient boiling water to cover it. Cover and cook for
    5 mins. Allow to stand for 5 mins, then discard the
    water.

2. Pour over sufficient boiling water to cover the
    gammon again. Cover and cook on HIGH (100%) for 10
    mins. Turn the joint over, cover and continue cooking
    on MEDIUM (50%) for about 45 mins, turning the
    gammon once, until cooked through.

3. Allow to stand for 10 mins, then drain off the stock
    (why not reserve it and make it into a delicious soup?).
    Cut the skin off the gammon and slash the fat lightly
    with a sharp knife (a striped or diamond pattern looks
    good).

4. Mix together the marmalade and sugar and spread the
    mixture over the fat surface. Cook under a hot grill
    until golden brown and bubbling hot.

LIVER AND APPLE CASSEROLE   *Serves 4*
Cooking time: about 20 mins

15g (¹/₂ oz) butter
1 medium onion, thinly sliced
1 medium carrot, thinly sliced
450g (1 lb) lamb's liver, thinly sliced
30ml (2 tbsp) flour
salt and freshly ground black pepper
2.5 ml (¹/₂ tsp) dried sage or
**   5ml (1 tsp) chopped fresh**
450ml (³/₄ pt) boiling lamb or beef stock
2 eating apples, cored and sliced

1. Put the butter, onion and carrot in a large bowl. Cover and cook for 5 mins, stirring once.

2. Add the liver. Stir in the flour, seasoning and sage. Gradually stir in the boiling stock. Cover and cook for 5 mins or until boiling.

3. Add the apples, cover and cook on MEDIUM (50%) for 5-10 mins, stirring once, until the liver is just tender.

CHICKEN 'ROAST' WITH GRAVY

Serves 6

Cooking time: about 40 mins

1 small onion, quartered
1 small lemon, quartered
1.6kg (3½ lb) oven-ready chicken
40g (1½ oz) butter
15ml (1 tbsp) paprika
30ml (2 tbsp) flour or cornflour
300ml (½ pt) hot chicken stock
30ml (2 tbsp) white wine or dry sherry
salt and freshly ground black pepper

1. Slip the onion and lemon quarters inside the chicken cavity and stand it on a microwave rack in a shallow dish.

2. Heat the butter for 45 secs or until melted and stir in the paprika. Brush half the mixture over the chicken.

3. Cover with a split microwave or roasting bag and cook on MEDIUM-HIGH (75%) for about 35 mins, turning the chicken over twice during cooking and brushing with the remaining butter mixture. The chicken is cooked when the juices run clear if the thick part of the leg is pierced with a sharp knife.

4. Lift the chicken on to a warmed serving plate, loosely cover with foil and leave to stand for 15 mins.

5. Meanwhile, skim off almost all the fat from the juices in the cooking dish. Stir the flour or cornflour into the juices and whisk until smooth. Gradually whisk in the stock and wine or sherry. Cook for 3-5 mins, whisking frequently, until the gravy thickens and boils. Season to taste.

6. Serve the gravy with the chicken.

CHICKEN WITH BARBECUE SAUCE   *Serves 4*
Cooking time: about 45 mins   ❄

1.4kg (3 lb) oven-ready chicken
15ml (1 tbsp) oil
1 small onion, finely chopped
60ml (4 tbsp) tomato ketchup
30ml (2 tbsp) Worcestershire sauce
30ml (2 tbsp) mango chutney, chopped if necessary
5ml (1 tsp) mustard powder
30ml (2 tbsp) lemon juice
5ml (1 tsp) sugar
salt and freshly ground black pepper

1. Brush the chicken with the oil and put it, breast side down, in a large shallow dish. Cover and cook on MEDIUM-HIGH (75%) for about 30 mins, turning the chicken over half way. It is cooked when the juices run clear if the thick part of the leg is pierced with a sharp knife.

2. Lift the chicken on to a warmed plate, loosely cover with foil and leave to stand for 15 mins.

3. Meanwhile, skim most of the fat off the juices in the dish. Stir the onion into the juices, cover and cook for 3 mins. Stir in the remaining ingredients, seasoning to taste. Cover and cook on MEDIUM (50%) for about 10 mins.

4. Carve the chicken and serve with the sauce poured over it.

CHICKEN IN MUSTARD SAUCE

Serves 4

Cooking time: about 25 mins

❊

15g (¹/₂ oz) butter
1 medium onion, thinly sliced
2 medium leeks, sliced
8 chicken thighs, skinned
150ml (¹/₄ pt) chicken stock
150ml (¹/₄ pt) dry white wine
30ml (2 tbsp) French mustard
salt and freshly ground black pepper
100g (4 oz) button mushrooms, sliced

1. Put the butter, onion and leeks in a large bowl. Cover and cook for 5 mins. Stir well.

2. Arrange the chicken in a circle on top of the vegetables.

3. Mix together the stock, wine, mustard and seasoning and stir in the mushrooms. Pour over the chicken.

4. Cover and cook on HIGH (100%) for 5 mins, then continue cooking on MEDIUM (50%) for about 15 mins, spooning the sauce over the chicken occasionally during cooking, until the chicken is tender.

CHICKEN IN ORANGE
Cooking time: about 15 mins

Serves 4
✳

10ml (2 tsp) oil
550g (1¹/₄ lb) boneless chicken breasts, skinned and
sliced
10ml (2 tsp) cornflour
grated rind and juice of 1 large orange
1 chicken or vegetable stock cube
15ml (1 tbsp) dark soy sauce
15ml (1 tbsp) clear honey
1 bunch of spring onions, sliced
salt and freshly ground black pepper
orange slices, to garnish

1. Put the oil and chicken into a medium bowl. Cover and cook for 5 mins, stirring once.

2. Blend the cornflour with the orange juice and the crumbled stock cube. Stir in the orange rind, soy sauce, honey and spring onions. Pour the sauce over the chicken.

3. Cover and cook for 5-10 mins, stirring occasionally, until the sauce thickens and boils and the chicken is tender.

4. Season to taste and serve, garnished with orange slices.

CHICKEN CHASSEUR

Cooking time: about 35 mins

Serves 4

❉

25g (1 oz) butter
1 medium onion, finely chopped
30ml (2 tbsp) flour
150ml (¹/₄ pt) dry white wine
300ml (¹/₂ pt) boiling chicken stock
salt and freshly ground black pepper
4 chicken breasts, skinned
100g (4 oz) button mushrooms
15ml (1 tbsp) chopped fresh parsley

1. Put the butter and onion in a large bowl, cover and cook for 3 mins.

2. Stir in the flour, then gradually stir in the wine. Add the boiling chicken stock, salt and pepper. Cook for 5 mins, stirring occasionally, or until the sauce thickens and boils.

3. Add the chicken to the sauce, coating it well. Cover and cook on MEDIUM (50%) for about 20 mins, stirring occasionally, until the chicken is tender.

4. Stir in the mushrooms and parsley, cover and cook for 3 mins. Leave to stand for 5 mins before serving.

CURRIED CHICKEN

Serves 4

Cooking time: about 20 mins ❄

10ml (2 tsp) oil
1 large onion, finely chopped
2 garlic cloves, crushed
4 boneless chicken breasts, skinned and thickly sliced
30ml (2 tbsp) curry paste
10ml (2 tsp) flour
15ml (1 tbsp) white wine vinegar
juice of 1 lemon
150ml (¼ pt) chicken stock
cooked rice, poppadums (see page 251) and
  mango chutney, to serve

1. Put the oil, onion and garlic into a medium bowl, cover and cook for 3 mins.

2. Stir in the chicken, cover and cook for 2 mins.

3. Blend the curry paste with the flour, vinegar and lemon juice. Stir into the stock and pour over the chicken.

4. Cover and cook on MEDIUM (50%) for about 15 mins, stirring occasionally, or until the chicken is tender.

5. Serve with rice, poppadums and mango chutney.

SPICED CHICKEN DRUMSTICKS

Serves 1

Cooking time: about 6 mins

❄

15ml (1 tbsp) tomato purée
10ml (2 tsp) French mustard
pinch of chilli powder
salt and freshly ground black pepper
2 chicken drumsticks

1. Put the first four ingredients into a small bowl and mix well. Brush the mixture over the drumsticks, coating them well. Arrange the drumsticks on a microwave rack on a plate, with thin ends to the centre, or with thin ends overlapping.

2. Cover with a sheet of microwave or non-stick paper and cook on MEDIUM-HIGH (75%) for about 6-7 mins or until the juices run clear when the thick part of the chicken is pierced with a sharp knife.

3. Leave to stand for a few mins before serving.

CHICKEN ORIENTAL

Serves 4

Cooking time: about 12 mins

10ml (2 tsp) oil
4 boneless chicken breasts, skinned and thinly sliced
15ml (1 tbsp) grated fresh root ginger
30ml (2 tbsp) soy sauce
30ml (2 tbsp) dry sherry
1 bunch of spring onions, sliced
2 red or yellow peppers (or one of each), seeds
    removed and thinly sliced
225g can water chestnuts, drained and sliced
30ml (2 tbsp) toasted sesame seeds
few drops of sesame oil

1. Put the oil and chicken in a large bowl and mix well. Cover and cook for 3 mins, stirring once.

2. Mix together the ginger, soy sauce and sherry and add to the bowl with the onions, peppers and water chestnuts.

3. Cover and cook for 6-10 mins, stirring occasionally, until the chicken is cooked through.

4. Stir in the sesame seeds and sesame oil before serving.

TURKEY 'ROAST' WITH
REDCURRANT SAUCE

Serves 4

Cooking time: about 20 mins

❄

550g (1¼ lb) pre-packed turkey roast, thawed if
  frozen
60ml (4 tbsp) redcurrant jelly
1 small onion, finely chopped
100g (4 oz) button mushrooms, thinly sliced
150ml (¼ pt) red wine
2.5ml (½ tsp) dried thyme
salt and freshly ground black pepper

1. Remove the turkey from its wrappings and put it in a
   casserole. Spread the redcurrant jelly over the turkey,
   cover and cook for 5 mins.

2. Turn the turkey over and spoon the juices over it.
   Cover and cook on MEDIUM (50%) for about 10 mins
   or until the juices run clear when the turkey is pierced
   with a sharp knife.

3. Lift the turkey on to a warmed serving plate, loosely
   cover with foil and leave to stand for 10 mins.

4. Meanwhile, stir the onion into the juices, cover and
   cook for 2 mins. Stir in the mushrooms, wine and
   thyme. Season to taste. Cover and cook for 2-3 mins.

5. Cut the turkey into 8 slices and arrange on the serving
   dish. Pour the sauce over and serve.

TURKEY IN TOMATO SAUCE WITH MUSHROOMS

Serves 4

Cooking time: about 30 mins

❊

45ml (3 tbsp) flour
salt and freshly ground black pepper
700g (1½ lb) boneless turkey fillet, cut into cubes
25g (1 oz) butter
1 large onion, finely chopped
1 garlic clove, crushed
150ml (¼ pt) chicken stock
150ml (¼ pt) dry white vermouth
400g can chopped tomatoes
225g (8 oz) button mushrooms
30ml (2 tbsp) chopped parsley

1. Season the flour with salt and pepper. Add the turkey and toss to coat it well.

2. Put the butter, onion and garlic into a large bowl. Cover and cook for 5 mins, stirring once.

3. Add the turkey to the onion mixture and stir in the stock, vermouth and tomatoes. Cover and cook for 15 mins, stirring once.

4. Stir in the mushrooms and cook, uncovered, for about 10 mins until the turkey is tender and the sauce has reduced slightly. Add the parsley just before serving.

FRUITED TURKEY CURRY

Serves 4

Cooking time: about 22 mins ❄

15g (1/2 oz) butter
1 medium onion, finely chopped
30ml (2 tbsp) curry powder
15ml (1 tbsp) flour
600ml (1 pt) hot chicken stock
15ml (1 tbsp) lemon juice
30ml (2 tbsp) Worcestershire sauce
30ml (2 tbsp) mango chutney
50g (2 oz) sultanas
1 medium eating apple, peeled, cored and sliced
salt and freshly ground black pepper
400g (14 oz) cooked turkey, cut into bite-size pieces

1. Put the butter and onion into a large casserole, cover and cook for 3 mins.

2. Stir in the curry powder and flour, then gradually blend in the stock. Cover and cook for about 5 mins or until boiling, stirring once or twice.

3. Add the remaining ingredients, except the turkey, and mix well. Cover and cook for 5 mins.

4. Stir in the turkey, cover and cook on MEDIUM (50%) for 8-10 mins.

DUCK WITH PLUM SAUCE

Serves 4

Cooking time: about 20 mins (plus marinating) ❄

30ml (2 tbsp) soy sauce
30ml (2 tbsp) red wine vinegar
30ml (2 tbsp) clear honey
1 garlic clove, crushed
2 large duck breasts, each weighing about 250g (10 oz);
   or 4 small ones, each weighing about 175g (6 oz)
467g can red plums in syrup
5ml (1 tsp) black treacle
5ml (1 tsp) tomato purée
5ml (1 tsp) arrowroot
salt and freshly ground black pepper

1. In a large bowl, mix together the soy sauce, vinegar, honey and garlic. Use a fork to pierce the duck in several places on both sides. Put the duck into the bowl, turning it to coat it well. Cover and leave to marinate for about 30 mins or (refrigerated) for several hours.

2. Drain the duck, reserving the marinade. Put the duck, skin side uppermost, on a microwave rack in a shallow dish. Lightly cover with kitchen paper and cook on MEDIUM (50%) for about 15 mins until the duck is just cooked. Leave to stand for 5 mins.

3. Meanwhile, drain the plums, reserving 30ml (2 tbsp) syrup, and remove the stones. Put the stoned plums into a blender or food processor. Add the reserved syrup and marinade, treacle, tomato purée and arrowroot. Purée until smooth. Pour into a jug or bowl and cook for about 4 mins or until boiling, stirring occasionally. Season to taste.

4. Thinly slice the duck and serve with the sauce.

10
Eggs and Cheese

Eggs and cheese are popular choices for a quick snack, breakfast, lunch or supper. Both do well in the microwave, so long as they are cooked gently and without overcooking.

HANDY HINTS - EGGS

- Do not try to cook an egg in its shell – steam builds up beneath the shell, making it explode, even after the microwaves have been switched off.

- Eggs which are at room temperature give the best results.

- Prick the yolks of eggs which are to be left whole during cooking, to prevent them from bursting open.

- Avoid overcooking eggs – they become tough. Always stop cooking before the egg or eggs are fully cooked – they will finish cooking during a short standing time.

- If eggs cook too quickly on HIGH (100%), better results may be achieved by using MEDIUM (50%).

HANDY HINTS - CHEESE

- Add cheese to a dish towards the end of cooking when possible, to prevent it overcooking and becoming stringy.

- Cheese melts quickly and evenly if it is grated rather than sliced or diced.

- If cheese cooks too quickly on HIGH (100%), better results may be achieved by using MEDIUM (50%).

BAKED EGGS

1. Break the eggs into small cups, dishes or ramekins. Prick the yolks. Arrange the dishes in a circle in the microwave.

2. Cook on MEDIUM (50%) until almost set:

   1 egg - about 1 min
   2 eggs - about 1½ mins
   3 eggs - about 2 mins
   4 eggs - about 2½ mins

3. Leave to stand for 1-2 mins before serving.

POACHED EGG

1. Pour 150ml (¼ pt) water into a medium bowl or jug. Add a dash of vinegar. Cook until boiling.

2. Break an egg into the boiling water. Prick the yolk.

3. Cook for ½-1 min.

4. Leave to stand for 1-2 mins until the egg is set. Lift out with a slotted spoon and serve.

SCRAMBLED EGGS   *Serves 2*
Cooking time: about 3 mins

4 eggs

60ml (4 tbsp) milk

25g (1 oz) butter

salt and freshly ground pepper

1. In a medium bowl or jug, beat together the eggs and milk. Add the butter and season to taste.

2. Cook for 2-3 mins, stirring or whisking frequently each time the egg sets around the edges of the bowl. Stop cooking when the eggs are still slightly undercooked – they will continue cooking as they are being served.

   Note: If you find the eggs cook too quickly on HIGH (100%), reduce the power to MEDIUM (50%) and cook for a little longer.

SCRAMBLED EGGS WITH HERBS AND GARLIC

Serves 1

Cooking time: about 3 mins

two size 2 eggs, beaten
salt and freshly ground black pepper
15ml (1 tbsp) milk
15g ($^1/_2$ oz) butter
40g (1$^1/_2$ oz) cream cheese with herbs and garlic

1. Put the eggs, seasoning, milk and butter into a bowl. Cook for 1 min, stirring once.

2. Crumble in the cheese and cook on MEDIUM (50%) for 2-3 mins, stirring frequently, or until the mixture is just set.

3. Serve immediately.

EGG AND LEEK BAKE

Serves 1

Cooking time: about 5 mins

1 small leek, thinly sliced
knob of butter
two size 2 eggs, beaten
pinch of ground mace
salt and freshly ground black pepper
10ml (2 tsp) snipped fresh chives

1. Put the leek and butter into a small shallow dish, cover and cook for 2-3 mins until soft.

2. Season the eggs with mace, salt and black pepper. Pour over the leeks.

3. Cook on MEDIUM (50%) for 1$^1/_2$-2 mins or until the eggs are just wet.

4. Sprinkle with chives and leave to stand for 1-2 mins before serving.

CHEESE BAKED EGGS

Serves 1

Cooking time: about 1¹/₂ mins (plus grilling if wished)

two size 2 eggs
1.25ml (¹/₄ tsp) dried dill or 2.5ml (¹/₂ tsp) chopped
    fresh dill
salt and freshly ground black pepper
25g (1 oz) grated Cheddar or Gruyère cheese

1. Break the eggs into two flameproof ramekins or small straight-sided dishes. Prick the yolks. Sprinkle the dill over each egg.

2. Cook both dishes on MEDIUM (50%) for 1-1¹/₂ mins or until the eggs are nearly set.

3. Season and sprinkle the cheese over.

4. Put under a hot grill until the cheese bubbles. Serve immediately.

EGG AND CHEESE ROLL

Serves 1

Cooking time: about 2 mins

1 soft bread roll
15g (¹/₂ oz) butter
1 egg
25g (1 oz) grated cheese

1. Cut a slice off the top of the bread roll and reserve. Scoop out the soft centre of the roll.

2. Put the butter in a small bowl and cook for 30 secs until melted. Brush some butter in the cavity of the roll. Brush the remainder over the cut side of the reserved slice.

3. Break the egg into the roll and prick the yolk. Sprinkle with grated cheese and replace the lid.

4. Cook, uncovered, for 1¹/₂-2 mins, or until the egg is just set. Serve hot or cold.

PIPERADE
Serves 2

Cooking time: about 8 mins

25g (1 oz) butter
1 small onion, finely chopped
1 garlic clove, crushed
1 medium green pepper, seeds removed and thinly
  sliced
227g can chopped tomatoes, drained
salt and freshly ground black pepper
4 eggs, beaten

1. Put the butter, onion, garlic and pepper in a medium bowl. Cover and cook for 5 mins.

2. Stir in the tomatoes and season to taste with salt and pepper. Cook, uncovered, for 1 min.

3. Stir in the eggs and cook, uncovered, for 2-3 mins, stirring frequently, until the eggs are lightly scrambled.

4. Serve immediately.

BACON AND MUSHROOM OMELETTE
Serves 2

Cooking time: about 7 mins

15g ($^{1}/_{2}$ oz) butter
2 lean bacon rashers, rinds removed and chopped
50g (2 oz) button mushrooms, thinly sliced
2 spring onions, chopped
4 eggs, beaten
salt and freshly ground black pepper

1. Put the butter and bacon in a shallow dish measuring about 20cm (8 in) in diameter. Cook, uncovered, for 2 mins.

2. Stir in the mushrooms and onions and cook, uncovered, for 1 min.

3. Season the eggs with salt and pepper and pour them over the bacon mixture. Cook, uncovered, for 3-4 mins, until just set, lifting the cooked areas from the sides of the dish after each minute to allow the liquid to run to the edges.

4. Cut into wedges to serve.

EGGS FLORENTINE

Serves 4

Cooking time: about 14 mins (plus grilling)

700g (1½ lb) fresh spinach, chopped
25g (1 oz) butter
45ml (3 tbsp) flour
300ml (½ pt) milk
75g (3 oz) mature Cheddar cheese, grated
salt and freshly ground black pepper
4 eggs

1. Put the spinach in a large bowl, cover and cook for 5 mins, stirring once, or until just tender. Drain well.

2. Put the butter, flour and milk in a medium bowl or jug and whisk well. Cook for about 5 mins, whisking frequently, until the sauce thickens and boils. Stir in the cheese and season with salt and pepper.

3. Break the eggs into four small dishes or ramekins and prick the yolks. Cook on MEDIUM (50%) for 3-4 mins, until the egg whites are just set.

4. Put the spinach in a shallow flameproof dish. Slide the eggs out of their dishes, on to the spinach. Pour the cheese sauce over and brown under a hot grill.

WELSH RAREBIT

Serves 1

Cooking time: about 2 mins

50g (2 oz) grated Cheddar cheese
15ml (1 tbsp) brown ale
1.25ml ($^1/_4$ tsp) mustard powder
knob of butter
salt and freshly ground black pepper
1 slice of hot toast

1. Put the cheese, ale, mustard and butter into a bowl and season. Cook on MEDIUM (50%) for about 2 mins or until melted, stirring once or twice.

2. Pour the mixture over the hot toast and serve immediately.

CHEDDAR FONDUE

Serves 4-6

Cooking time: about 8 mins

1 garlic clove, halved
450g (1 lb) mature Cheddar cheese, grated
15ml (1 tbsp) cornflour
300ml ($^1/_2$ pt) white wine
5ml (1 tsp) lemon juice
25g (1 oz) butter
freshly ground pepper
pinch of ground nutmeg
crusty bread cubes, to serve

1. Rub the inside of a large bowl with the cut sides of the garlic.

2. Add the cheese and cornflour to the bowl and mix well. Stir in the wine, lemon juice and butter.

3. Cook, uncovered, for 6-8 mins, stirring frequently, until the cheese melts and the mixture is thick and smooth.

4. Season with pepper and stir in the nutmeg.

5. Serve with bread cubes – let each person spear them on long forks and dip into the fondue.

CHEESE PUDDING

Serves 4

Cooking time: about 20 mins (plus grilling if wished)

225g (8 oz) fresh breadcrumbs
225g (8 oz) grated Cheddar cheese
600ml (1 pt) milk
40g (1½ oz) butter
three size 2 eggs, beaten
pinch of mustard powder
salt and freshly ground black pepper

1. Mix the breadcrumbs with 175g (6 oz) cheese and tip the mixture into a buttered 1.1 litre (2 pt) soufflé dish.

2. Put the remaining ingredients in a bowl or jug and mix well. Cook for 1-2 mins until the butter has melted. Pour over the breadcrumb mixture and sprinkle the remaining cheese over the top.

3. Cook on MEDIUM-LOW (30%) for 15-20 mins or until the pudding is set, turning the dish occasionally. The pudding is cooked when a knife inserted in the centre comes out clean.

4. If wished, lightly brown the top of the pudding under a hot grill.

11

Vegetables

Fresh vegetables cooked in the microwave are simply delicious. Because they are cooked quickly and in the minimum amount of liquid, they retain their full flavour and colour, and cook to the stage where they are still slightly crunchy. Small quantities of vegetables are very successful too, cooked in a small dish so there is no saucepan to wash up.

Cooked vegetables also reheat well in the microwave – to look and taste freshly cooked.

HANDY HINTS - VEGETABLES

● Use good quality vegetables for best results. Old, tired vegetables will not improve on cooking.

● Choose even-sized vegetables for cooking whole. Otherwise, cut them into even-sized pieces to encourage even cooking.

- Prick the skins of whole vegetables in several places before cooking, to prevent them bursting open.

- Frozen vegetables can be cooked straight from the freezer. Follow the packet instructions.

- Arrange whole vegetables in a circle, to encourage them to cook evenly. Avoid putting one in the centre.

- When cooking more than 450g (1 lb) cut vegetables, best results may be obtained if they are cooked in batches.

- Add 45-60ml (3-4 tbsp) water to the vegetables. Root vegetables and old vegetables often need more. Extra water may also be needed if you want to cook vegetables until they are very soft.

- Season vegetables with salt after cooking or they will become dry and tough.

- Cook most vegetables on HIGH (100%). If they tend to overcook or shrivel, it may be preferable to cook on a slightly lower power, such as MEDIUM-HIGH (75%) or even MEDIUM (50%).

- Cover cut vegetables during cooking to keep the moisture in.

- Stir, shake or turn vegetables occasionally to encourage them to cook evenly.

- Cooking times will depend on the type and quantity of vegetables as well as their age. As a guide, 450g (1 lb) cut vegetables take 7-10 mins. Always underestimate the time and test in the usual way – by inserting the tip of a knife.

- Leave whole vegetables, such as potatoes,to stand for several minutes before serving, to allow the temperature to even out.

BLANCHING VEGETABLES

1. Put up to 450g (1 lb) prepared vegetables in a bowl with 45-60ml (3-4 tbsp) water.

2. Cover and cook for 3-4 mins, stirring once, until the vegetables are hot.

3. Quickly drain and tip the vegetables into ice-cold water. Drain them again, then put into polythene bags and freeze.

JACKET POTATOES

1. Scrub and dry potatoes weighing about 175g (6 oz) each. Using a fork, prick their skins in several places. Put them in the microwave, in a circle.

2. Cook, uncovered, until tender:
   5-6   mins for 1
   8-10   mins for 2
   9-12   mins for 3
   10-15 mins for 4.
   Turn them over at least once during cooking.

3. Leave the potatoes to stand for 5 mins before serving.

LAYERED POTATOES

Serves 4

Cooking time: about 25 mins (plus grilling)

butter
450g (1 lb) potatoes, thinly sliced
1 medium onion, thinly sliced
salt and freshly ground black pepper
2.5ml (¹/₄ tsp) ground mace or nutmeg
300ml (¹/₂ pt) milk or single cream
50g (2 oz) grated Cheddar cheese

1. Butter a flameproof dish. Layer the potatoes and onion in the dish, lightly seasoning each layer. Whisk the mace into the milk or cream and pour over the potatoes. Dot with butter.

2. Cover and cook on MEDIUM (50%) for about 25 mins or until the potatoes are tender.

3. Sprinkle with cheese and brown under a hot grill before serving.

POTATOES DAUPHINOIS
Serves 4

Cooking time: about 30 mins (plus grilling)

15g ($\frac{1}{2}$ oz) butter, plus extra for the dish
700g ($1\frac{1}{2}$ lb) potatoes, thinly sliced
50g (2 oz) Cheddar or Gruyère cheese, grated
salt and freshly ground black pepper
150ml ($\frac{1}{4}$ pt) double cream
150ml ($\frac{1}{4}$ pt) milk
1 garlic clove, crushed
pinch of ground nutmeg

1. Butter a flameproof dish. Layer the potatoes with the cheese in the dish, seasoning each layer lightly.

2. Mix the cream with the milk and add the garlic and nutmeg. Pour evenly over the potatoes. Dot with the butter.

3. Cover and cook for 5 mins.

4. Uncover and cook on MEDIUM (50%) for about 25 mins until the potatoes are tender.

5. Brown under a hot grill

PARSLEY BAKED ONIONS
Serves 4

Cooking time: about 12 mins

350g (12 oz) small or pickling onions, peeled
5ml (1 tsp) lemon juice or white wine vinegar
25g (1 oz) butter
45ml (3 tbsp) chopped fresh parsley
salt and freshly ground black pepper

1. Put all the ingredients in a medium bowl, cover and cook for 10-12 mins until soft, stirring occasionally.

2. Leave to stand for 5 mins before serving.

MUSHY SPLIT PEAS

Serves 4-6

Cooking time about: 30 mins (plus soaking) ❇

225g (8 oz) split yellow peas
1 small onion, finely chopped
750ml (1¼ pt) hot bacon stock
freshly ground black pepper
25g (1 oz) butter

1. Put the peas in a large bowl and pour over sufficient boiling water to cover them well. Leave to stand for 1 hour.

2. Drain the peas and put them into a very large casserole. Stir in the onion and hot stock and season with pepper. Cover and cook on HIGH (100%) for about 10 mins until boiling. Then continue to cook on MEDIUM (50%) for about 15 mins or until the peas are tender, stirring occasionally.

3. Thicken the mixture if necessary by uncovering the casserole and cooking on HIGH (100%) so that the peas boil rapidly, and the mixture reduces and thickens.

4. Stir in the butter before serving.

CHANTILLY PEAS

Serves 4

Cooking time: about 8 mins

25g (1 oz) butter
225g (8 oz) frozen peas
100g (4 oz) frozen carrots
15ml (1 tbsp) lemon juice
45ml (3 tbsp) double cream or crème fraîche
15ml (1 tbsp) chopped fresh mint
salt and freshly ground black pepper

1. Put the butter in a bowl and cook for about 45 secs until melted. Stir in the peas and carrots, cover and cook for 5-6 mins, stirring once. Leave to stand for 5 mins.

2. Stir in the remaining ingredients, cover and cook for 1-2 mins.

STUFFED TOMATO

Serves 1

Cooking time: about 4 mins

1 medium beef tomato
4 spring onions, sliced
pinch of garlic granules
5ml (1 tsp) oil
$^1/_2$ medium green pepper, seeds removed and chopped
15g ($^1/_2$ oz) raisins
15g ($^1/_2$ oz) chopped walnuts
1.25-2.5ml ($^1/_4$-$^1/_2$ tsp) curry powder or garam masala
dash of Worcestershire sauce
15g ($^1/_2$ oz) bran flakes
salt and freshly ground black pepper

1. Slice the top off the tomato, scoop out the centre and roughly chop the scooped-out pieces.

2. Put the onions, garlic, oil, pepper and raisins into a bowl. Cover and cook for 2 mins.

3. Stir in the walnuts, curry powder, Worcestershire sauce, bran flakes and chopped tomato. Season with salt and black pepper. Cook for 1 min.

4. Pile the mixture into the tomato shell, top with its lid and put on a plate. Cook for about 1 min.

5. Leave to stand for 1-2 mins before serving.

CORN ON THE COB WITH GARLIC BUTTER

Cooking time: about 7 mins ·*Serves 1*

25g (1 oz) butter
1 garlic clove, crushed
1 medium cob of corn
5ml (1 tsp) chopped fresh parsley or other fresh herb

1. Put half the butter into a small bowl and add the garlic. Cook for about 30 secs or until melted.

2. Brush the butter mixture over the corn, coating it well, then wrap it in microwave or non-stick paper.

3. Put the parcel on a plate and cook for 5-6 mins or until just tender, turning it over once.

4. Leave to stand for a few mins before opening the parcel, sprinkling the parsley over the corn and topping with the remaining butter.

5. Serve immediately.

CARROTS IN ORANGE GLAZE
Serves 4

Cooking time: about 10 mins

450g (1 lb) carrots, thinly sliced
25g (1 oz) butter
75ml (5 tbsp) orange juice
5ml (1 tsp) clear honey
salt and freshly ground black pepper
15ml (1 tbsp) chopped fresh parsley

1. Put the carrots in a large bowl and add the butter, orange juice and honey. Cover and cook for about 10 mins, stirring occasionally, until the carrots are tender.

2. Season to taste and stir in the parsley.

LEEKS PARMESAN
Serves 4

Cooking time: about 14 mins (plus grilling if wished)

✻ *omit breadcrumbs and cheese*

50g (2 oz) butter
50g (2 oz) fresh breadcrumbs
25g (1 oz) Parmesan cheese, finely grated
4 medium leeks, thinly sliced
5ml (1 tsp) soft brown sugar
30ml (2 tbsp) double cream
salt and freshly ground black pepper

1. Put 25g (1 oz) butter in a shallow ovenproof dish and cook for 30 secs or until melted. Stir in the breadcrumbs, coating them well. Cook, uncovered, for about 4 mins, stirring frequently, until golden brown. Add the cheese.

2. Put the remaining butter, leeks and sugar in a bowl. Cover and cook for about 8 mins, stirring occasionally, until the leeks are just tender.

3. Stir in the cream and season to taste. Cook for 1 min.

4. Tip the leeks and their sauce into a flameproof dish and scatter the breadcrumb mixture over the top. If wished, brown under a hot grill for a few minutes before serving.

LEEKS IN HAM WITH CHEESE SAUCE

Cooking time: about 15 mins   *Serves 4*

❄

40g (1¹/₂oz) butter
4 medium leeks, trimmed to about 15cm (6 in) long
salt and freshly ground black pepper
25g (1 oz) flour
300ml (¹/₂ pt) milk
pinch of ground nutmeg
1 egg, beaten
4 lean ham slices
50g (2 oz) grated Cheddar cheese

1. Put the butter in a flameproof dish and cook for about 1 min until melted. Arrange the leeks in the dish (leave a small space between them) and brush them with the butter. Sprinkle with black pepper.

2. Cover and cook for about 8 mins, turning them once and brushing again with the butter.

3. Lift the leeks out of the butter and set aside.

4. Stir the flour into the butter and gradually stir or whisk in the milk. Season with salt and add the nutmeg. Cook for 2-3 mins, whisking frequently, until the sauce thickens and boils. Leave to cool slightly then quickly stir in the egg.

5. Wrap each leek in a slice of ham and push them into the sauce, spooning it over the top. Cook on MEDIUM (50%) for about 3 mins until heated through.

6. Brown under a hot grill before serving.

BROCCOLI IN HAM AND CHEESE SAUCE

Cooking time: about 7 mins   *Serves 1*
(plus grilling if wished)

100g (4 oz) small broccoli florets
15g (¹/₂ oz) flour
150ml (¹/₄ pt) milk
15g (¹/₂ oz) butter
2.5ml (¹/₂ tsp) ready-made mustard
1 ham slice, cut into thin strips
15ml (1 tbsp) grated Parmesan cheese
freshly ground black pepper

1. Put the broccoli into a bowl with 30ml (2 tbsp) water, cover and cook for about 4 mins, stirring once, or until it is just tender. Leave to stand.

2. Meanwhile, put the flour in a jug or bowl and gradually whisk in the milk. Add the butter and mustard. Cook for 2-3 mins, whisking frequently, until the sauce thickens and boils. Stir in the ham and cheese (reserving a little). Season to taste.

3. Drain the broccoli and arrange it in a flameproof dish. Pour the sauce over it. Sprinkle with the reserved cheese and brown under a hot grill if wished.

BEETROOT AND APPLE SALAD

Serves 4

Cooking time: about 15 mins   ✽

225g (8 oz) beetroot, diced
30ml (2 tbsp) red wine vinegar
5ml (1 tsp) sugar
2 celery sticks, thinly sliced
1 large eating apple, cored and diced

1. Put the beetroot, vinegar and sugar in a medium bowl with 60ml (4 tbsp) water. Cover and cook for about 15 mins, stirring occasionally, or until the beetroot is tender.

2. Stir in the celery and apples. Serve warm or chilled.

GINGERED CABBAGE

Serves 4

Cooking time: about 10 mins

40g (1¹/₂ oz) butter
15ml (1 tbsp) grated fresh root ginger
1 small garlic clove, crushed
450g (1 lb) cabbage, shredded
salt and freshly ground black pepper

1. Put the butter in a large bowl and cook for 45 secs or until melted.

2. Stir in the ginger and garlic. Add the cabbage and stir well to coat it with butter.

3. Cover and cook for about 9 mins, stirring occasionally, or until tender.

4. Season to taste before serving.

VEGETABLES IN CREAM SAUCE

Serves 2 as a main meal, 4 as an accompaniment
Cooking time: about 10 mins

25g (1 oz) butter
1 large onion, thinly sliced
4 medium carrots, thinly sliced
4 celery sticks, thinly sliced
225g (8 oz) small broccoli florets
100g (4 oz) button mushrooms
150ml (¼ pt) vegetable stock
15ml (1 tbsp) cornflour
150ml (¼ pt) soured cream
salt and freshly ground black pepper
15ml (1 tbsp) chopped fresh chives
50g (2 oz) toasted cashew nuts or pine nuts

1. Put the butter and onion in a large bowl, cover and cook for 3 mins.

2. Stir in the carrots, celery, broccoli, mushrooms and stock. Cover and cook for about 8 mins, stirring occasionally, until the vegetables are just tender.

3. Mix the cornflour with the cream to make a smooth paste, season to taste and add the chives. Stir into the vegetables. Cook, uncovered, for about 2 mins, stirring once, until the sauce thickens and boils.

4. Scatter the nuts over the top and serve immediately.

CURRIED VEGETABLES

Serves 4

Cooking time: about 20 mins

❄

30ml (2 tbsp) oil
10ml (2 tsp) ground coriander
5ml (1 tsp) ground cumin
2.5ml ($^1\!/_2$ tsp) turmeric
2.5ml ($^1\!/_2$ tsp) chilli powder
1 medium onion, finely chopped
2 garlic cloves, crushed
2 medium potatoes, chopped
2 medium carrots, sliced
1 small cauliflower, cut into small florets
227g can tomatoes
150ml ($^1\!/_4$ pt) vegetable stock
2 medium courgettes, thickly sliced
50g (2 oz) creamed coconut, chopped
salt and freshly ground black pepper
150ml ($^1\!/_4$ pt) natural yoghurt
cooked rice, to serve

1. Put the oil, spices, onion and garlic in a large bowl, cover and cook for 3 mins, stirring once.

2. Add the potatoes, carrots and cauliflower. Stir well to coat them with the spices.

3. Mix the tomatoes with the vegetable stock and add to the bowl.

4. Cover and cook for about 12 mins, stirring gently occasionally.

5. Add the courgettes and coconut, cover and cook for 5 mins, gently stirring once or twice, until the coconut has melted and the vegetables are tender.

6. Season to taste, stir in the yoghurt and serve with rice.

RATATOUILLE

Cooking time: about 30 mins

Serves 4-6
❈

1 medium aubergine, sliced
salt
30ml (2 tbsp) olive oil
1 large onion, thinly sliced
1 large garlic clove, crushed
2 large courgettes, sliced
1 red pepper, seeds removed and sliced
1 yellow pepper, seeds removed and sliced
400g can chopped tomatoes
30ml (2 tbsp) chopped fresh herbs, such as thyme,
   basil and/or parsley
30ml (2 tbsp) tomato purée
salt and freshly ground black pepper

1. Sprinkle the aubergine slices with salt, if wished, and allow to stand for 30 mins. Rinse and dry well.

2. Put the oil, onion and garlic in a large bowl. Cover and cook for 5 mins, stirring once.

3. Stir in the aubergine slices, courgettes and peppers. Cover and cook for 5 mins, stirring once.

4. Add the tomatoes, herbs and tomato purée. Season well. Cover and cook for 5 mins on HIGH (100%), then continue cooking on MEDIUM (50%) for 15 mins, stirring gently occasionally.

5. Allow to stand for at least 10 mins before serving hot or cold.

VEGETABLE STIR FRY WITH CASHEW NUTS
Cooking time: about 6 mins   *Serves 2*

15g (¹/₂ oz) butter
1 garlic clove, crushed
100g (4 oz) carrots, thinly sliced
1 red, yellow or green pepper, seeds removed and
    thinly sliced
2 celery sticks, thinly sliced
100g (4 oz) button mushrooms, thickly sliced
4 spring onions, sliced
30ml (2 tbsp) light soy sauce
30ml (2 tbsp) dry sherry
pinch of five-spice powder
5ml (1 tsp) sugar
5ml (1 tsp) cornflour
50g (2 oz) cashew nuts, toasted

1. Put the butter, garlic and carrots into a large bowl, cover and cook for 3 mins.

2. Stir in the remaining vegetables, cover and cook for 2 mins.

3. Whisk together the soy sauce, sherry, five-spice powder, sugar and cornflour and stir into the vegetable mixture. Cover and cook for about 2 mins until the sauce has thickened and the vegetables are just tender.

4. Serve topped with the cashew nuts.

CHILLI BEANS

Serves 4

Cooking time: about 15 mins

10ml (2 tsp) oil
1 medium onion, finely chopped
1 garlic clove, crushed
420g can butter beans, drained
439g can kidney beans, drained
420g can chick peas, drained
450g can baked beans in tomato sauce
400g can chopped tomatoes
2 vegetable stock cubes
30ml (2 tbsp) tomato purée
5ml (1 tsp) chilli powder, or to taste
freshly ground black pepper
50g (2 oz) grated Cheddar cheese, to serve

1. Put the oil, onion and garlic into a large bowl, cover and cook for 3 mins.

2. Stir in the butter and kidney beans, chick peas, baked beans and tomatoes. Crumble in the stock cubes and stir in the tomato purée, and add chilli powder and pepper.

3. Cook for about 10 mins, stirring twice.

4. Serve in warmed bowls, topped with cheese.

MIXED BEAN MEDLEY

Serves 4-6

Cooking time: about 17 mins   ❅

30ml (2 tbsp) olive oil

1 large onion, thinly sliced

2 garlic cloves, crushed

15ml (1 tbsp) tomato purée

45ml (3 tbsp) chopped fresh herbs, such as thyme, oregano, and/or fennel

5ml (1 tsp) sugar

227g can chopped tomatoes

grated rind and juice of 1 lemon

430g can haricot beans, drained

439g can red kidney beans, drained

salt and freshly ground black pepper

green salad and garlic bread, to serve

1. Put the oil, onion and garlic in a large bowl, cover and cook for 3 mins.

2. Mix together the tomato purée, herbs, sugar, tomatoes, lemon rind and juice. Pour over the onion, cover and cook for 4 mins, stirring once, or until boiling.

3. Stir in the beans and season to taste. Cover and cook on MEDIUM (50%) for about 10 mins.

4. Serve hot or at room temperature with salad and garlic bread.

BUTTER BEAN POT

Serves 1

Cooking time: about 10 mins (plus grilling)

15g (¹/₂ oz) butter
1 small onion, finely chopped
¹/₂ green pepper, seeds removed and finely chopped
227g can chopped tomatoes with herbs
15ml (1 tbsp) tomato purée
220g can butter beans, drained
1 egg
100g (4 oz) curd cheese
25g (1 oz) grated mature Cheddar cheese

1. Put the butter, onion and pepper in a bowl, cover and cook for about 3 mins until soft.

2. Stir in the tomatoes, cover and cook for about 3 mins.

3. Stir in the tomato purée and then the beans. Spoon into a flameproof dish.

4. Lightly beat the egg and add the curd cheese, stirring until smooth. Stir in half the grated cheese. Spoon the mixture over the beans and scatter the remaining cheese over the top.

5. Cover and cook on MEDIUM (50%) for about 5 mins until set. Lightly brown under a hot grill and serve immediately.

PARSNIP AND ONION BAKE

Serves 4

Cooking time: about 12 mins (plus grilling) ❄

225g (8 oz) onions, thinly sliced
225g (8 oz) parsnips, thinly sliced
salt and freshly ground black pepper
30ml (2 tbsp) chopped fresh parsley
45ml (3 tbsp) white wine or water
25g (1 oz) flour
300ml (½ pt) milk
15g (½ oz) butter
1 egg, beaten

1. Arrange half the onions in the base of a flameproof dish. Arrange half the parsnips on top. Season with salt and pepper and sprinkle over half the parsley. Repeat the layers, finishing with the parsley. Sprinkle over the wine or water.

2. Cover and cook for about 8 mins or until the parsnips are tender. Leave to stand.

3. Meanwhile, put the flour into a bowl or jug and blend in a little milk to make a smooth paste. Gradually whisk in the remaining milk. Season with salt and pepper and add the butter. Cook for 3-4 mins, whisking frequently, until the sauce thickens and boils. Leave the sauce to cool slightly, then quickly stir in the egg.

4. Spread the sauce over the parsnip mixture and brown under a hot grill.

12

Rice, Pasta, Pulses, Cereals and Grains

Cooking rice, pasta and pulses is not necessarily quicker in a microwave. However, if it's not being used for other cooking, the microwave is certainly convenient.

Instant breakfast cereals and porridge are quick and convenient too, particularly when individual portions are prepared in the microwave.

HANDY HINTS - RICE, PASTA AND PULSES

● Use a large deep bowl, to allow the contents to boil up.

● Adding a little oil to the cooking water helps to prevent pasta from boiling over.

● Large quantities, over 450g (1 lb), are best cooked in batches or conventionally on the hob.

● Always add boiling water to the rice, pasta or pulses. Boil the water in the kettle to save time.

- Salt can be added to the cooking water of pasta. Rice and pulses are best seasoned with salt after cooking, to prevent them from toughening.

- Though covering during cooking keeps moisture in, results are just as good if no cover is used - and there is less chance of the contents boiling over and flooding the floor of the microwave

- Stir well after adding the boiling water before cooking.

- Rice need not be stirred again, but pasta and pulses should be stirred occasionally during cooking.

- Leave to stand for 5 minutes before serving.

RICE – Basic method
1. Put the rice in a large deep bowl. Pour over boiling water:
    300ml ($\frac{1}{2}$ pt) for 100g (4 oz) white rice
    450ml ($\frac{3}{4}$ pt) for 100g (4 oz) brown rice
    600ml (1 pt) for 225g (8 oz) white rice
    750ml ($1\frac{1}{4}$ pt) for 225g (8 oz) brown rice.

2. Stir well. Cook for about 10 mins for white rice, or 20-30 mins for brown rice, or until the rice is tender and has absorbed very nearly all the water.

3. Season to taste, stir, cover and leave the rice to stand for 5 mins before fluffing it up with a fork and serving.

PASTA – Basic method

1. Put the pasta in a large deep bowl with salt and a little oil, if wished. Pour over sufficient boiling water to cover the pasta by at least 2.5cm (1 in). Stir well.

2. Cook for:
   > 3-4 mins for 225g (8 oz) fresh pasta
   > 7-10 mins for 225g (8 oz) dried pasta
   > 10-14 mins for 450g (1 lb) dried pasta.

   Stir occasionally during cooking, to prevent the pasta pieces sticking together. Stop cooking when the pasta is still slightly undercooked.

3. Stir well, cover and leave to stand for 5 mins before draining and serving.

PULSES – Basic method

1. Soak 225g (8 oz) pulses in plenty of cold water overnight. Alternatively, pour plenty of boiling water over the pulses, cover and allow to stand for 1-2 hours. (Split peas and lentils do not need soaking before cooking.)

2. Drain and put the pulses into a large bowl and pour over enough boiling water to cover them by at least 2.5cm (1 in).

3. Cook, stirring occasionally, until tender.
   > *Aduki beans:* 30-35 mins
   > *Black-eye beans:* 25-35 mins
   > *Cannellini beans:* 30-45 mins
   > *Chick peas:* 50-60 mins
   > *Flageolet beans:* 35-45 mins
   > *Haricot beans:* 25-35 mins
   > *Lentils:* 20-30 mins
   > *Mung beans:* 20-30 mins
   > *Peas:* 30-45 mins
   > *Red kidney beans:* 30-45 mins
   > *Split peas:* 20-30 mins.

4. Cover and leave to stand for 5 mins before draining and using.

POLENTA

Serves 4

Cooking time: about 10 mins

100g (4 oz) instant polenta
pinch of salt
50g (2 oz) butter
freshly grated Parmesan cheese (optional)

1. Put the polenta and salt into a medium bowl. Gradually add 600ml (1 pt) boiling water, stirring continuously until smooth.

2. Cook for 8-10 mins, stirring occasionally.

3. Stir in the butter, and if using, Parmesan cheese to taste. Serve immediately.

COUSCOUS

Serves 2

Cooking time: about 4 mins

100g (4 oz) couscous
pinch of salt
15ml (1 tbsp) olive oil

1. Put the couscous into a medium bowl with 300ml ($\frac{1}{2}$ pt) boiling water. Stir in the salt and oil.

2. Cook for about 4 mins, then cover and leave to stand for 5 mins.

3. Use as required.

BULGAR WHEAT
Cooking time: about 5 mins

Serves 2

100g (4 oz) bulgar (burghul or cracked) wheat
pinch of salt

1. Put the wheat in a medium bowl with 300ml (½ pt) boiling water. Stir in the salt.

2. Cook for about 5 mins, then leave to stand for 5 mins.

3. Use as required.

PORRIDGE
Cooking time: about 4 mins

Serves 2

50g (2 oz) porridge oats
300ml (½ pt) milk
salt, sugar, or honey

1. Put the oats in a medium bowl and add the milk. Cook, uncovered, for about 4 mins or until the porridge thickens and boils, stirring frequently.

2. Add salt, sugar or honey to taste.

PILAU RICE

Serves 3-4

Cooking time: about 10 mins

225g (8 oz) basmati rice
15ml (1 tbsp) oil
4 green cardamoms
4 whole cloves
1 cinnamon stick
2.5ml (¹/₂ tsp) cumin seeds
1.25ml (¹/₄ tsp) ground turmeric

1. Put the rice into a sieve and wash well under cold running water. Drain.

2. Put the oil and spices into a large bowl and stir. Cook for about 1 min, stirring once.

3. Add the rice, stirring to coat it with the spices. Add 600ml (1 pt) boiling water and stir.

4. Cook, uncovered, for 8-10 mins until the rice is just tender.

5. Cover and leave to stand for 3 mins before fluffing up with a fork and serving.

VEGETABLE RISOTTO

Serves 4

Cooking time: about 25 mins

15ml (1 tbsp) oil
25g (1 oz) butter
1 large leek, finely sliced
1 garlic clove, crushed
175g (6 oz) arborio or risotto rice
600ml (1 pt) vegetable stock
150ml (¹/₄ pt) dry white vermouth
225g (8 oz) small broccoli florets
225g (8 oz) button mushrooms
grated Parmesan cheese, to serve

1. Put the oil, butter, leek and garlic in a large bowl, cover and cook for 5 mins, stirring once.

2. Stir in the rice, cover and cook for 2 mins.

3. Add the stock and vermouth. Cook, uncovered, for 10 mins.

4. Stir in the broccoli and mushrooms and cook, uncovered, for about 8 mins.

5. Cover and leave to stand for 5 mins. Serve, sprinkled with Parmesan cheese.

LEEK AND MUSHROOM RISOTTO   *Serves 1*
Cooking time: about 20 mins

15g ('/₂ oz) butter
1 small leek, thinly sliced
50g (2 oz) risotto or long grain rice
300ml ('/₂ pt) hot vegetable or chicken stock
60ml (4 tbsp) dry white vermouth
50g (2 oz) small button mushrooms
25g (1 oz) toasted flaked almonds
grated Parmesan or Cheddar cheese, to serve

1. Put the butter into a medium bowl and cook for about 30 secs until melted.

2. Stir the leek and rice into the butter, cover and cook for 1 min.

3. Stir in the hot stock and vermouth. Cook, uncovered, on HIGH (100%) for about 2 mins or until boiling, then continue cooking on MEDIUM (50%) for about 15 mins or until the rice is tender and it has absorbed almost all the liquid.

4. Stir in the mushrooms and almonds. Cook, uncovered, for 1 min.

5. Serve immediately with some Parmesan or Cheddar cheese sprinkled over the top or stirred into the risotto.

TURKEY PILAFF

Serves 4

Cooking time: about 25 mins

25g (1 oz) butter
50g (2 oz) flaked almonds
10ml (2 tsp) oil
1 medium onion, finely sliced
100g (4 oz) button mushrooms
225g (8 oz) long grain rice
600ml (1 pt) boiling chicken stock
25g (1 oz) raisins
4 turkey breast fillets, cut into thick strips

1. Put the butter in a shallow ovenproof dish and cook for 30 secs until melted. Add the almonds and cook for 3 mins, stirring frequently, until golden brown. Drain on kitchen paper.

2. Pour any excess butter from the almonds into a large bowl. Add the oil, onion and mushrooms, cover and cook for 3 mins.

3. Stir in the rice and cook for 2 mins.

4. Add the boiling stock and raisins. Stir in the turkey, pushing the pieces under the surface of the stock.

5. Cover and cook for 10 mins, stirring occasionally. Uncover and cook for a further 5 mins or until the turkey is cooked through.

6. Scatter the almonds over the top to serve.

VEGETABLE PAELLA

Serves 3-4

Cooking time: about 25 mins

30ml (2 tbsp) olive oil
1 medium onion, sliced
1 garlic clove, crushed
1 large green pepper, seeds removed and sliced
1 large red pepper, seeds removed and sliced
1 medium carrot, thinly sliced
1 medium leek, thinly sliced
50g (2 oz) frozen peas
50g (2 oz) frozen green beans
225g (8 oz) arborio or risotto rice
1.25ml ($\frac{1}{4}$ tsp) ground turmeric
600ml (1 pt) hot vegetable stock
salt and freshly ground black pepper

1. Put the oil, onion and garlic into a large bowl, cover and cook for about 5 mins, stirring once.

2. Stir in the vegetables, cover and cook for 5 mins, stirring once.

3. Add the rice and turmeric, pour over the hot vegetable stock and season with a little salt and plenty of pepper. Stir well.

4. Cook uncovered for about 12 mins or until the stock has been absorbed and the rice is tender.

5. Cover and leave to stand for about 3 mins before serving.

LASAGNE

Serves 4

Cooking time: about 45 mins (plus grilling) ❈

Note: best results are obtained if the recipe is made up to the end of stage 5 and left to stand, refrigerated, for several hours or overnight.

5ml (1 tsp) oil
1 medium onion, finely chopped
1 garlic clove, crushed
350g (12 oz) lean minced beef or lamb
1 beef or lamb stock cube
15ml (1 tbsp) dried oregano
30ml (2 tbsp) tomato purée
400g can chopped tomatoes
salt and freshly ground black pepper
25g (1 oz) butter
25g (1 oz) flour
300ml (½ pt) milk
100g (4 oz) mature Cheddar cheese, grated
6 sheets no-pre-cook lasagne
25g (1 oz) Parmesan cheese, grated

1. Put the oil, onion and garlic in a large bowl, cover and cook for 5 mins, stirring once.

2. Crumble the beef or lamb and add to the bowl. Cover and cook for 5 mins, stirring twice.

3. Crumble in the stock cube and add the oregano, tomato purée, tomatoes and seasoning. Cover and cook for 12 mins, stirring occasionally.

4. Put the butter, flour and milk in a bowl or jug, and whisk. Cook, uncovered, for about 4 mins, whisking frequently, until the sauce thickens and boils. Stir in the Cheddar cheese.

5. Grease a shallow rectangular flameproof dish. Put a little

sauce in the bottom and top with half the lasagne sheets. Cover them with half the meat sauce then half the cheese sauce. Repeat the layers and scatter the Parmesan cheese over the top.

6. Cover and cook on MEDIUM (50%) for about 20 mins until the pasta is tender.

7. Brown the top of the lasagne under a hot grill.

MACARONI CHEESE

Serves 4

Cooking time: about 14 mins (plus grilling) ❄

225g (8 oz) macaroni
40g (1¹/₂ oz) butter
40g (1¹/₂ oz) flour
2.5ml (¹/₂ tsp) mustard powder
600ml (1 pt) milk
175g (6 oz) Cheddar cheese, grated
salt and freshly ground black pepper

1. Put the macaroni in a large bowl and pour over enough boiling water to cover it by 2.5cm (1 in). Stir well. Cook, uncovered, for 8 mins, stirring occasionally. Leave to stand.

2. Meanwhile, put the butter, flour, mustard powder and milk into a medium bowl or jug and whisk well. Cook for about 6 mins, whisking frequently, until the sauce thickens and boils. Stir in 100g (4 oz) cheese and season to taste with salt and pepper.

3. Drain the macaroni and stir it into the sauce. Pour the mixture into a flameproof dish and sprinkle with the remaining cheese.

4. Brown under a hot grill.

TUNA AND TOMATO PASTA

Serves 2

Cooking time: about 15 mins

175-225g (6-8 oz) pasta shapes
1 small onion, finely sliced
1 garlic clove, crushed
5ml (1 tsp) oil
230g can chopped tomatoes
5ml (1 tsp) lemon juice
salt and freshly ground black pepper
200g can tuna, drained

1. Cook the pasta, following the basic method on page 184. Cover and leave to stand.

2. Put the onion, garlic and oil into a medium bowl. Cover and cook for 3 mins.

3. Stir in the tomatoes, lemon juice and seasoning. Cook for 2 mins.

4. Roughly flake the tuna and stir in. Cook for 2-3 mins or until just bubbling, stirring once.

VEGETABLE PASTA

Serves 1

Cooking time: about 10 mins

75g (3 oz) pasta shapes
4 spring onions, sliced
100g (4 oz) courgettes, sliced
50g (2 oz) celery, thinly sliced
1 vegetable stock cube
10ml (2 tsp) soy sauce
30ml (2 tbsp) single cream
salt and freshly ground black pepper
grated Parmesan or Cheddar cheese, to serve

1. Put the pasta into a deep bowl and cover well with boiling water. Cook, uncovered, for 5-6 mins, stirring occasionally, or until almost tender. Leave to stand for a few mins.

2. Meanwhile, put the onions, courgettes and celery into a bowl. Dissolve the stock cube in 100ml (4 fl oz) boiling water and stir into the vegetables. Cover and cook for about 4 mins or until just tender, stirring once.

3. Drain the pasta and add the vegetables, soy sauce and cream. Toss lightly and season to taste.

4. Serve immediately, topped with Parmesan or Cheddar cheese.

PASTA WITH CHICKEN IN VERMOUTH

Cooking time: about 25 mins   *Serves 2*

225g (8 oz) pasta shapes
5ml (1 tsp) olive oil
1 medium onion, thinly sliced
5ml (1 tsp) sugar
1 boneless chicken breast, skinned and thinly sliced
150ml (¼ pt) dry white vermouth
300ml (½ pt) chicken stock
10ml (2 tsp) tomato purée
5ml (1 tsp) dried mixed herbs
10ml (2 tsp) cornflour

1. Cook the pasta followng the Basic Method on page 184. Cover and leave to stand.

2. Meanwhile, put the oil, onion and sugar into a bowl, cover and cook for 3 mins, stirring once.

3. Stir the chicken into the onion, cover and cook for 1 min.

4. Whisk together the vermouth, stock, tomato purée, herbs and cornflour. Pour over the chicken and stir well. Cook for about 12 mins, stirring occasionally, until the sauce thickens and boils.

5. Drain the pasta and serve topped with the chicken and its sauce.

SPINACH AND CHEESE CANNELLONI

Serves 1

Cooking time: about 10 mins (plus grilling if wished)

3 cannelloni tubes
5ml (1 tsp) oil
50g (2 oz) frozen spinach, thawed and drained
25g (1 oz) ricotta, curd or cream cheese
good pinch of ground mace
salt and freshly ground black pepper
3 spring onions, thinly sliced
230g can chopped tomatoes
knob of butter
10ml (2 tsp) chopped fresh basil or 5ml (1 tsp) dried
25g (1 oz) grated Cheddar cheese

1. Put the cannelloni and oil in a deep bowl and cover well with boiling water. Cook, uncovered, for 3-4 mins, stirring once, or until just soft. Drain and leave until cool enough to handle.

2. Meanwhile, mix the spinach into the ricotta, curd or cream cheese. Add the mace and season well. Use a teaspoon to spoon the spinach mixture into the cannelloni tubes. Arrange the filled tubes in a shallow flameproof dish.

3. Put the remaining ingredients (except the Cheddar cheese) into a small bowl. Cover and cook for 3 mins, stirring once.

4. Season the tomato sauce and pour it over the cannelloni, coating it well. Sprinkle with the Cheddar cheese. Cook, uncovered, for 1-2 mins until hot. If wished, brown under a hot grill before serving.

TAGLIATELLI WITH CHEESE AND WALNUT SAUCE

Serves 1

Cooking time: about 6 mins

50g (2 oz) green tagliatelli
45ml (3 tbsp) curd cheese
1 spring onion, thinly sliced
10ml (2 tsp) chopped fresh parsley
1 small garlic clove, crushed
15ml (1 tbsp) chopped fresh basil
15ml (1 tbsp) chopped walnuts
30ml (2 tbsp) single or double cream
freshly ground black pepper

1. Put the pasta into a deep bowl and cover well with boiling water. Cook, uncovered, for 5-6 mins, stirring occasionally, or until almost tender. Leave to stand for a few mins.

2. Meanwhile, put the remaining ingredients into a bowl and stir well.

3. Drain the tagliatelli, pour the sauce over and toss lightly until well mixed.

4. Serve immediately.

POLENTA WITH TOMATO SAUCE   *Serves 4*

Cooking time: about 15 mins (plus Tomato Sauce and, if wished, grilling)

100g (4 oz) instant polenta
pinch of salt
25g (1 oz) butter
1 quantity of Tomato Sauce (page 92)
30-45ml (2-3 tbsp) freshly grated Parmesan cheese

1. Put the polenta and salt into a medium bowl. Gradually add 600ml (1 pt) boiling water, stirring continuously until smooth. Stir in the butter.

2. Cook for 8-10 mins, stirring occasionally.

3. Spoon the mixture into a buttered shallow dish and level the top. Leave to cool completely.

4. (Meanwhile, make the Tomato Sauce.)

5. Cut the polenta into cubes and arrange in a lightly buttered shallow flameproof dish. Pour over the Tomato Sauce, cover and cook on MEDIUM (50%) for about 5 mins or until hot throughout.

6. Sprinkle with the cheese and, if wished, brown under a hot grill.

DHAL

Serves 2 as a main dish, 4 as a side dish
Cooking time: about 25 mins   ❉

1 medium onion, finely chopped
2 garlic cloves, crushed
15ml (1 tbsp) oil
5ml (1 tsp) sugar
2.5ml ($^1/_2$ tsp) grated fresh root ginger
1.25ml ($^1/_4$ tsp) ground cumin
1.25ml ($^1/_4$ tsp) turmeric
1.25ml ($^1/_4$ tsp) chilli powder
100g (4 oz) red lentils
450ml ($^3/_4$ pt) hot vegetable stock
finely grated rind and juice of $^1/_2$ a lemon
salt and freshly ground black pepper
chopped fresh coriander, to serve

1. Put the onion, garlic, oil, sugar, ginger and spices into a medium bowl. Cover and cook for 4 mins.

2. Stir in the lentils and hot stock. Cover and cook on MEDIUM-HIGH (75%) for about 20 mins, stirring occasionally, or until the lentils are soft.

3. Add the lemon rind and juice and season with salt and pepper. If wished, purée in a blender or food processor until smooth.

4. Serve sprinkled with coriander.

TWO-BEAN SALAD

Serves 4-6

Cooking time: about 15 mins

30ml (2 tbsp) olive oil
1 large red or white onion, thinly sliced
1 large garlic clove, crushed
10ml (2 tsp) sugar
230g can chopped tomatoes
grated rind and juice of 1 large lemon
30ml (2 tbsp) chopped fresh thyme or oregano
430g can red kidney beans, drained
430g can cannellini or haricot beans, drained

1. Put the oil, onion and garlic into a medium bowl, cover and cook for 4 mins, stirring once.

2. Add the sugar, tomatoes, lemon rind and juice and thyme or oregano. Stir, cover and cook for about 4 mins or until boiling, stirring once.

3. Stir in the beans, cover and cook on MEDIUM (50%) for about 7 mins.

4. Serve hot or at room temperature.

BULGAR WHEAT SALAD

Serves 4-6

Cooking time: about 5 mins

225g (8 oz) bulgar (burghul or cracked) wheat
600ml (1 pt) boiling vegetable stock
30ml (2 tbsp) olive oil
grated rind and juice of 1 small lemon
1 bunch spring onions, thinly sliced
half a cucumber, diced
4 tomatoes, skinned and chopped
60ml (4 tbsp) chopped fresh mint
60ml (4 tbsp) chopped fresh parsley
salt and freshly ground black pepper
10 black olives, pitted
fresh crusty bread, to serve

1. Put the bulgar wheat in a large bowl, stir in the boiling stock, cover and cook for 5 mins. Cover and leave to stand for 15 mins.

2. Add the oil, lemon rind and juice, onions, cucumber, tomatoes, mint and parsley. Season to taste with salt and pepper. Gently stir until well mixed, then tip into a large serving bowl.

3. Halve the olives and scatter over the salad. Serve at room temperature with crusty bread.

13

Desserts

Fruit is perfect for cooking in the microwave, staying in shape and retaining all its juice, flavour and colour. Light sponge and suet puddings are cooked in minutes instead of taking hours of steaming on the hob. Crumbles, cheesecakes, milk puddings and egg custard are all ideal candidates for microwave cooking too, and don't forget to use the microwave to dissolve gelatine and to melt chocolate for mousses and other desserts (see Chapter 16).

HANDY HINTS – FRUIT

● Pierce or split the skins of whole fruits, such as apples, to prevent them bursting open.

● Frozen fruit can be cooked straight from the freezer.

● Add water to hard fruits and fruits with thick skins, such as apples and plums. 45-60ml (3-4 tbsp) is a good guide.

- Soft fruits, such as raspberries and blackcurrants; fruits with a high water content, such as rhubarb; and apple slices for a purée, usually need no additional liquid.

- Either dissolve sugar in the cooking liquid, or add sugar after cooking. Do not sprinkle sugar over fruits with skins, such as plums or blackcurrants, or the skins will toughen.

- Cover during cooking, to keep the moisture in and to help the fruit cook evenly.

- Most fruit can be cooked on HIGH (100%), but if it tends to overcook or burst open, try lowering the power to MEDIUM (50%). The difference in the cooking time will be minimal.

- Cooking times depend on the type, quantity and age of the fruit. As a guide:
    450g (1 lb) soft fruit takes 2-5 mins
    450g (1 lb) hard fruit takes 7-10 mins.

- Stir gently or reposition whole fruit occasionally during cooking.

- Allow to stand for 3-5 mins before serving.

HANDY HINTS – SPONGE AND SUET PUDDINGS
- When cooking a conventional recipe in the microwave, add extra liquid to the mixture. About an extra 15ml (1 tbsp) per egg is a good guide.

- Use a pudding bowl which is large enough to allow the pudding to rise up.

- A transparent bowl allows you to see when the pudding is cooked.

- Lightly grease the bowl before adding the pudding mixture.

- Cover the pudding loosely with a 'hat' of microwave, greaseproof or non-stick paper – to keep moisture in and to allow the pudding to rise above the top of the bowl if necessary.

- Stand the bowl on a microwave rack to encourage even cooking.

- Cook on MEDIUM-HIGH (75%) for 3-7 mins, depending on the size of pudding.

- It's easy to overcook puddings. Stop cooking when the surface of the pudding is still slightly moist, but the mixture beneath it is cooked. The surface will dry as the pudding stands.

- Leave to stand for 3-5 mins to let it settle before turning the pudding out.

- Turn the pudding on to a warmed plate. (If you stand the pudding on a heatproof plate during cooking, the plate warms up ready for serving.)

- If the bottom of the pudding is still slightly undercooked, do not put it back into its bowl. Put the plated pudding back into the microwave and cook briefly until set.

HANDY HINTS - MILK PUDDINGS

- Use a large deep bowl, to allow the pudding to boil up.

- Cook, uncovered, on HIGH (100%) until the mixture boils, then continue cooking on MEDIUM (50%) or MEDIUM-LOW (30%) until the pudding is cooked: semolina, tapioca and ground rice take about 10 mins; whole rice takes 30-45 mins.

- Stir occasionally during cooking.

BAKED APPLES

Serves 4

Cooking time: about 6 mins

4 cooking apples, each weighing about 225-275g (8-10 oz), cored
90-120ml (6-8 tbsp) mincemeat

1. Using a small sharp knife, make a shallow cut through the skin around the middle of each apple.

2. Arrange the apples in a shallow dish and add 30ml (2 tbsp) water. Cover and cook for 3 mins.

3. Fill the apple centres with mincemeat. Cover and cook for 2-4 mins until the apples are tender. Should any of the apples cook too fast and threaten to burst open, you may prefer to reduce the microwave power level to MEDIUM (50%) and continue cooking until the apples are tender.

PEARS IN CIDER

Serves 4

Cooking time: about 13 mins

8 small pears, peeled
300ml (½ pt) sweet cider
30ml (2 tbsp) demerara sugar
2.5ml (½ tsp) almond essence

1. Arrange the pears, sitting them upright, around the edge of a shallow dish. Add the cider and sugar.

2. Cover and cook for about 10 mins until the pears are tender, spooning the juice over them occasionally during cooking. Carefully lift the pears on to a serving dish.

3. Return the juices to the microwave and cook, uncovered, for 2-3 mins until slightly reduced. Add the almond essence and pour the sauce over the pears.

4. Serve hot or chilled.

HONEY-BAKED BANANAS

Serves 4

Cooking time: about 6 mins

25g (1 oz) butter
juice of 1 medium orange
15ml (1 tbsp) clear honey
4 medium bananas
whipped cream or ice cream, to serve

1. Put the butter, orange juice and honey in a shallow dish. Cook for 2 mins until the butter has melted. Stir well.

2. Skin the bananas and halve them lengthways. Add to the dish, turning to coat them well with the butter mixture.

3. Cook for 3-4 mins until the bananas just begin to bubble.

4. Serve with whipped cream or ice cream.

TROPICAL BANANA

Serves 1

Cooking time: about 1¹/₂ mins

1 medium banana, peeled and thickly sliced
5ml (1 tsp) lemon or lime juice
1 small orange, peeled and segmented
knob of butter
5-10ml (1-2 tsp) demerara sugar
10ml (2 tsp) desiccated coconut
15ml (1 tbsp) raisins
15ml (1 tbsp) pineapple juice

1. Put the banana into a bowl and sprinkle over the lemon or lime juice, stirring gently. Add the orange segments and butter. Mix together the remaining ingredients and add to the banana mixture.

2. Cover and cook for 1-1¹/₂ mins.

3. Serve immediately.

ORANGES IN CARAMEL
Serves 1

Cooking time: about 5 mins

45ml (3 tbsp) orange juice
5ml (1 tsp) rum (optional)
15ml (1 tbsp) sultanas or raisins
25g (1 oz) caster sugar
1 medium orange

1. Put the orange juice, rum (if using) and sultanas into a small bowl. Cover and cook for 1 min.

2. Put the sugar into another bowl and add 45ml (3 tbsp) water. Cook for 1 min. Stir well until the sugar has completely dissolved. Cook, stirring every 30 secs, until the mixture just begins to turn a pale golden brown (take care not to overcook it). Leave to cool for a few mins.

3. Gradually stir the fruit mixture into the cooled sugar mixture.

4. Peel the orange, discarding pith and any seeds. Slice and arrange in a dish. Pour the syrup over.

5. Serve hot or chilled.

SPICY FRUIT COMPOTE
Serves 4

Cooking time: about 8 mins

250g packet dried fruit salad
5ml (1 tsp) vanilla extract
1 cinnamon stick
5 whole cloves
50g (2 oz) caster sugar

1. Put the fruit into a large bowl with 300ml (½ pt) boiling water. Add the vanilla, cinnamon stick and cloves.

2. Cover and cook for about 8 mins.

3. Stir in the sugar, cover and leave to stand for about 30 mins.

4. Serve hot, warm or chilled.

APPLE AND BLACKBERRY CRUMBLE
Cooking time: about 12 mins   *Serves 4*

450g (1 lb) cooking apples, peeled, cored and sliced
30ml (2 tbsp) sugar
225g (8 oz) fresh or frozen blackberries
75g (3 oz) block (hard) margarine
175g (6 oz) plain flour
75g (3 oz) demerara sugar

1. Put the apples and sugar in a 20.5cm (8 in) soufflé dish with 15ml (1 tbsp) water. Cover and cook for 3 mins.

2. Stir in the blackberries. Cover and cook for 2 mins.

3. Rub the margarine into the flour until the mixture resembles fine breadcrumbs. Stir in the sugar. Spoon the mixture on top of the fruit and level the surface.

4. Cook, uncovered, for about 7 mins. Leave to stand for a few mins before serving.

RICE PUDDING   *Serves 4*
Cooking time: about 50 mins (plus grilling if wished)

50g (2 oz) pudding rice
600ml (1 pt) milk
25g (1 oz) sugar
freshly grated nutmeg
15g (¹/₂ oz) butter

1. Put the rice, milk and sugar into a large bowl. Sprinkle with nutmeg and add the butter.

2. Cook for about 7 mins, stirring twice, or until boiling. Cover and cook on MEDIUM-LOW (30%) for 30-45 mins, stirring occasionally, until thick and creamy.

3. If wished, pour the pudding into a flameproof dish and brown lightly under a hot grill.

SEMOLINA PUDDING

Serves 4

Cooking time: about 15 mins

600ml (1 pt) milk
60ml (4 tbsp) semolina
15ml (1 tbsp) caster sugar, plus extra
15g (¹/₂ oz) butter

1. Put the milk into a large bowl and whisk in the semolina and sugar. Add the butter.

2. Cook, uncovered, for about 5 mins or until just boiling. Stir well.

3. Cover and cook on MEDIUM-LOW (30%) for about 10 mins, stirring frequently, until cooked and thickened.

4. Leave the pudding to stand for 5 mins before serving.

MACARONI PUDDING

Serves 4

Cooking time: about 25 mins (plus grilling if wished)

175g (6 oz) macaroni
600ml (1 pt) milk
40g (1½ oz) caster sugar
25g (1 oz) butter

1. Put all the ingredients into a large bowl. Cook, uncovered, on HIGH (100%) for about 5 mins or until just boiling. Stir well, then continue cooking, uncovered, on MEDIUM-LOW (30%) for about 20 mins, stirring occasionally, or until the macaroni is tender and the pudding has thickened slightly.

2. Leave to stand for 5 mins before serving.

3. If wished, transfer to a flameproof dish and lightly brown the top under a hot grill.

EGG CUSTARD

Serves 4

Cooking time: about 20 mins

3 eggs
25g (1 oz) caster sugar
600ml (1 pt) milk
freshly grated nutmeg

1. Lightly beat the eggs and sugar, then gradually beat in the milk. Strain the mixture into a dish, and sprinkle with nutmeg.

2. Stand the dish inside a larger container with sufficient boiling water to come half way up the dish.

3. Cook, uncovered, on MEDIUM (50%) for 15-20 mins until just set. Leave to stand for 5 mins before serving.

APRICOT UPSIDE-DOWN PUDDING
Cooking time: about 11 mins   *Serves 6*

411g can apricot halves in fruit juice
25g (1 oz) butter
25g (1 oz) soft brown sugar
150g (5 oz) soft margarine
150g (5 oz) caster sugar
2 eggs, beaten
175g (6 oz) self-raising flour, sieved

1. Drain the apricots, reserving 75ml (5 tbsp) of the juice.

2. Put the butter in a 20.5cm (8 in) soufflé dish and cook for 45 secs or until melted. Brush the base and sides of the dish with the butter, then scatter the brown sugar on to the buttered surface. Arrange the apricots in the base of the dish.

3. Beat the margarine and caster sugar together until light and fluffy. Add the eggs, a little at a time, beating well after each addition. Fold in the flour and reserved fruit juice.

4. Spoon the pudding mixture over the apricots and level the surface.

5. Place the dish on a microwave rack and cook, uncovered, for about 10 mins until the surface is still slightly moist but the pudding beneath it is cooked.

6. Leave to stand for 5 mins before turning out on to a warmed plate.

PINEAPPLE UPSIDE-DOWN PUDDING
Follow the recipe above, replacing the apricots with a 411g can pineapple slices.

SYRUP SPONGE PUDDING

Serves 4

Cooking time: about 7 mins

30ml (2 tbsp) golden syrup
50g (2 oz) margarine
50g (2 oz) caster sugar
1 egg, beaten
100g (4 oz) self-raising flour
few drops of vanilla extract
45ml (3 tbsp) milk

1. Butter a 600ml (1 pt) pudding basin and spoon the syrup in the bottom.

2. Put the margarine, sugar, egg, flour and vanilla extract in a bowl and beat well until smooth. Gradually stir in the milk. Spoon the mixture on top of the syrup and level the surface.

3. Cover loosely with a 'hat' of greaseproof paper and place the pudding on a microwave rack. Cook on MEDIUM-HIGH (75%) for 6-8 mins until the surface is still slightly moist but the pudding beneath it is cooked. Leave to stand for 5 mins before turning out on to a warmed plate.

SINGLE-SERVE SPONGE PUDDING
WITH JAM SAUCE

Serves 1

Cooking time: about 3 mins

40g (1½ oz) self-raising flour
25g (1 oz) soft margarine
25g (1 oz) caster sugar
one size 4 egg, beaten
few drops of vanilla extract
10ml (2 tsp) milk
30ml (2 tbsp) jam
few drops of lemon juice

1. Put the flour, margarine, sugar, egg, vanilla extract and milk into a bowl and beat until smooth. Spoon the mixture into a lightly-greased teacup or bowl. Level the top.

2. Cover with a 'hat' of microwave or non-stick paper and cook on MEDIUM-HIGH (75%) for about 2 mins or until the pudding is still slightly moist on top but the mixture beneath it is cooked.

3. Leave to stand for 2 mins.

4. Meanwhile, put the jam into a small jug or bowl with 10ml (2 tsp) water and the lemon juice. Cook on MEDIUM (50%) for 1-1½ mins until the jam has melted. Stir well.

5. Turn the pudding on to a warmed serving plate and pour the jam sauce over. Serve immediately.

SUET PUDDING WITH JAM

Serves 4

Cooking time: about 10 mins

butter
30ml (2 tbsp) jam
100g (4 oz) self-raising flour
pinch of salt
50g (2 oz) caster sugar
50g (2 oz) shredded suet
1 egg, beaten
milk

1. Butter a 900ml (1½ pt) pudding bowl and spoon the jam into it.

2. Sift the flour and salt into a bowl and stir in the sugar, suet, egg and sufficient milk to make a soft consistency.

3. Spoon the mixture on top of the jam and cover with a 'hat' of microwave or non-stick paper.

4. Cook on MEDIUM (50%) for 7-10 mins or until the surface of the pudding springs back into shape when pressed lightly.

5. Leave to stand for about 5 mins before turning out on to a warmed serving plate. Serve immediately.

BREAD AND BUTTER PUDDING   *Serves 4*
Cooking time: about 18 mins (plus grilling if wished)

butter
6 bread slices, lightly buttered
45ml (3 tbsp) sultanas, raisins or chopped dates
450ml ($^3/_4$ pt) milk
two size 2 eggs
40g (1$^1/_2$ oz) caster sugar

1. Lightly butter a straight-sided dish. Cut the buttered bread into triangles and arrange them, overlapping, in the dish. Scatter the dried fruit over the top, allowing some to fall down between the bread.

2. Put the milk in a jug and cook for 2-3 mins until very hot but not quite boiling.

3. Beat the eggs with the sugar, then whisk in the hot milk. Strain (through a sieve) over the bread. Leave to stand for 30 mins.

4. Put the dish into a large container and pour round sufficient boiling water to come half way up the sides of the dish. Cook on MEDIUM (50%) for about 15 mins or until just set,

5. If wished, lightly brown under a hot grill before serving.

BREAD PUDDING

Serves 4

Cooking time: about 20 mins (plus standing and, if wished, grilling)

225g (8 oz) fresh bread, cut into small pieces
300ml (½ pt) milk
50g (2 oz) butter
one size 2 egg, beaten
10ml (2 tsp) ground mixed spice
50g (2 oz) dried mixed peel
175g (6 oz) dried mixed fruit
Demerara sugar

1. Put the bread into a bowl and pour the milk over. Leave to soak for 10-20 mins.

2. Put the butter into a small bowl and cook for 1-2 mins until melted.

3. Stir the butter, egg, spice, peel and fruit into the bread mixture, and spoon it into a lightly buttered, straight-sided dish.

4. Cook, uncovered, on MEDIUM (50%) for about 10 mins until just firm.

5. Leave to stand for 10 mins.

6. Continue cooking on MEDIUM (50%) for about 10 mins.

7. If wished, lightly brown the top under a hot grill.

8. Sprinkle Demerara sugar over the top and leave to stand for at least 10 mins.

9. Serve hot or cold.

QUEEN OF PUDDINGS
Cooking time: about 8 mins

Serves 4

450ml (¾ pt) milk
two size 2 eggs, separated
50g (2 oz) caster sugar
grated rind of half a lemon
25g (1 oz) butter
75g (3 oz) fresh breadcrumbs
30ml (2 tbsp) jam

1. Put the milk, egg yolks, 25g (1 oz) sugar and lemon rind into a jug and whisk well. Add the butter. Cook for about 3 mins, stirring once.

2. Stir the breadcrumbs into the milk mixture and tip into a lightly buttered straight-sided dish.

3. Put the jam into a small bowl and cook for 30 secs until soft and runny. Trickle it over the breadcrumb mixture.

4. Whisk the egg whites to make soft peaks, then fold in the remaining sugar. Spoon the meringue on top of the jam.

5. Cook, uncovered, on MEDIUM (50%) for 3-4 mins or until set.

6. If wished, lightly brown under a hot grill before serving.

7. Serve hot, warm or cold.

BISCUIT CRUMB
Sufficient to line the base of two 20.5cm (8 in) dishes
Cooking time about: 2 mins

Use as base for cheesecake or for chilled creams and jellies.

❋ shaped into bases

225g (8 oz) crunchy sweet biscuits
75g (3 oz) butter
25-50g (1-2 oz) sugar (optional)

1. Put the biscuits in a strong polythene food bag and crush with a rolling pin to make small crumbs.

2. Put the butter in a bowl and cook for 1-2 mins until melted. Stir in the biscuits and, if wished, sweeten the mixture by stirring in some sugar.

3. Press half the mixture into the base of a 20.5cm (8in) flan dish. Repeat with the other half.

4. Chill until firm, then use as required.

BLACKCURRANT CHEESECAKE

Serves 6

Cooking time: about 9 mins

❄

50g (2 oz) butter
100g (4 oz) digestive biscuits, crushed
175g (6 oz) soft cream cheese
100g (4 oz) cottage cheese
2 eggs, beaten
30ml (2 tbsp) caster sugar
5ml (1 tsp) cornflour
397g can blackcurrant pie filling

1. Put the butter in a bowl and cook for 1 min until melted. Add the biscuits and stir well. Press the mixture into the base of the flan dish.

2. Put the cream cheese, cottage cheese, eggs, sugar and cornflour into a blender or processor and purée until smooth. Pour on to the biscuit base.

3. Cook, uncovered, on MEDIUM (50%) for about 8 mins or until set (don't worry if the centre is still slightly moist - this will set as the cheesecake cools).

4. Leave to cool before spreading the pie filling over the top of the cheesecake.

WHITE CHOCOLATE MOUSSE

Serves 4-6

Cooking time: about 5 mins   ❄

175g (6 oz) white chocolate
15ml (1 tbsp) clear honey
5ml (1 tsp) gelatine
150ml (¹/₄ pt) whipping cream
2 egg whites
25g (1 oz) white or plain chocolate, to decorate

1. Break the white chocolate into a small bowl. Add 45ml (3 tbsp) water and the honey. Cook on MEDIUM-LOW (30%) for about 4 mins. Stir well until melted and smooth.

2. Put 45ml (3 tbsp) water in another small bowl and sprinkle the gelatine over. Leave it to stand for 1 min. Cook on HIGH (100%) for 30-45 secs, stirring every 15 secs, until clear (make sure it does not boil). Stir into the white chocolate.

3. Whip the cream until it stands in soft peaks. Fold it into the chocolate mixture.

4. Using a clean bowl and whisk, whisk the egg whites until stiff. Fold into the chocolate mixture. Spoon into 4-6 small glasses and chill until set.

5. To decorate, chill the remaining chocolate, then make chocolate shavings by drawing a potato peeler across it. Sprinkle some on the top of each mousse.

CHOCOLATE MOUSSE

Serves 4

Cooking time about: 4 mins ✳

Use really fresh eggs for this. Since the egg yolks are not fully cooked, this recipe is not suitable for those at risk from salmonella.

225g (8 oz) plain chocolate
40g (1½ oz) butter
4 eggs, separated
20ml (4 tsp) rum
whipped cream and grated chocolate, to decorate

1. Break the chocolate into a bowl and add the butter. Cook on MEDIUM (50%) for about 4 mins, stirring occasionally, until melted.

2. Beat in the egg yolks and rum. Whisk the egg whites until stiff and fold them into the chocolate mixture.

3. Spoon into 4 serving dishes or glasses and chill for about 2 hours until set.

4. Decorate with whipped cream and grated chocolate to serve.

14

Cakes, Biscuits and Sweets

Cakes cooked in the microwave rise well and their flavour is good. Their texture is slightly pudding-like and they do not brown and crisp (though a combination cooker, which browns while it microwaves, will bake some cakes successfully). Generally, very moist mixtures are suited to microwave cooking, as are recipes in which the fats and sugars are melted together. The microwave recipes in this section have been tried and tested over the years.

Some biscuit recipes can be microwaved but because they can only be cooked in small batches, and need frequent attention, it is more convenient to cook them conventionally. However, shortbread and flapjacks are successful and I have included the recipes for these, together with microwave meringues.

Remember, the microwave makes speedy work of melting butter, chocolate, and so on, for sweets - a few recipes are included.

HANDY HINTS - CAKES

● Choose circular dishes with straight, not sloping, sides. Ring moulds produce the most successful cakes, with no chance of the centre remaining uncooked.

● When trying a recipe for the first time, choose a deep container – cakes rise considerably during cooking. Half fill it only.

● Lightly grease the cooking container. Do not coat it with flour or a disagreeable crust will form on the outside of the cake.

● Line the base of the container with microwave, non-stick or greased greaseproof paper, for easy removal of the cake.

● When cooking a conventional recipe in the microwave, add extra liquid to the mixture – about an extra 15ml (1 tbsp) per egg is a good guide. Fruit cakes should have a very soft dropping consistency (see page 227).

● Plump up dried fruit before adding it to a cake mixture (see method on page 227).

● Sugar must be well blended into the mixture – lumps of sugar attract microwaves and burn easily.

● Small cakes should be arranged in a circle in the microwave, with the centre left free.

● Sit the dish on a microwave rack to make sure the cake cooks evenly.

● Cook sponge-type cakes on HIGH (100%) and fruit cakes on MEDIUM (50%) or MEDIUM-LOW (30%). Check with your oven manufactuer's instruction book too.

- It's easy to overcook cakes, causing them to stale quickly. Stop cooking when the surface of the cake is still slightly moist but the mixture beneath it is cooked. The surface will dry out as it stands. The cake is cooked when a wooden cocktail stick inserted in the centre comes out clean.

- Leave to stand before turning the cake out – 5 mins for sponge-type cakes and 20 mins for fruit cakes.

- Turn the cake out on to a cooling rack lined with non-stick paper – to prevent it sticking to the rack.

CHOCOLATE CAKE
Cooking time: about 7 mins

Serves 6-8
❄

200g (7 oz) self-raising flour
5ml (1 tsp) baking powder
2.5ml ($^1/_2$ tsp) bicarbonate of soda
30ml (2 tbsp) cocoa powder
75g (3 oz) caster sugar
2 eggs, beaten
150ml ($^1/_4$ pt) corn or sunflower oil
150ml ($^1/_4$ pt) milk
30ml (2 tbsp) golden syrup

1. Grease a 20.5cm (8 in) cake or soufflé dish and line its base with a circle of microwave or non-stick paper.

2. Sift the flour, baking powder, bicarbonate of soda and cocoa into a medium bowl. Stir in the sugar.

3. Whisk together the eggs, oil, milk and syrup. Add to the dry ingredients and beat well until smooth. Pour the mixture into the prepared dish.

4. Sit the dish on a microwave rack. Cook for 6-7 mins until the surface is still slightly moist but the cake beneath it is cooked.

5. Leave to stand for 10 mins before turning the cake out on to a cooling rack lined with non-stick paper.

LEMON SPONGE RING

Serves 8

Cooking time: about 7 mins

❄

150g (5 oz) caster sugar, plus extra for coating
175g (6 oz) self-raising flour
5ml (1 tsp) baking powder
175g (6 oz) soft margarine
3 eggs, beaten
300ml (2 tbsp) lemon curd
Topping:
60ml (4 tbsp) lemon juice
45ml (3 tbsp) caster sugar
crystallised lemon slices

1. Grease a medium ring mould and lightly coat the greased surface with the extra caster sugar.

2. Sieve the flour with the baking powder.

3. Beat the margarine and 150g (5 oz) caster sugar together until light and fluffy. Add the eggs, a little at a time, beating well after each addition. Fold in the flour mixture.

4. Put the lemon curd into a small bowl and cook for 45 secs until melted. Stir into the cake mixture with 30ml (2 tbsp) warm water. Pour into the prepared ring mould.

5. Cook for about 6 mins until the surface is still slightly moist but the cake beneath it is cooked.

6. Leave to stand for 2-3 mins before turning the cake out on to a cooling rack lined with non-stick paper.

7. To make the topping, mix the lemon juice with the caster sugar and pour over the warm cake. Decorate with lemon slices and leave to cool.

FRUIT CAKE RING

Serves 16

Cooking time: about 55 mins

❄

500g (1 lb 2 oz) mixed dried fruit
150ml (¹/₄ pt) orange or apple juice
250g (9 oz) plain flour
5ml (1 tsp) ground mixed spice
5ml (1 tsp) ground ginger
5ml (1 tsp) ground nutmeg
175g (6 oz) butter, softened
175g (6 oz) soft dark brown sugar
4 eggs
30ml (2 tbsp) black treacle
50g (2 oz) walnuts, chopped
100g (4 oz) glacé cherries, chopped
45ml (3 tbsp) milk

1. Grease a 2 litre (3¹/₂ pt) ring mould and line its base with microwave or non-stick paper.

2. Put the fruit and orange or apple juice in a bowl, cover and cook for 5 mins until plumped up and soft.

3. Sieve the flour with the spice, ginger and nutmeg. Beat the butter and sugar together until light and fluffy. Add the eggs, one at a time, beating and adding 15ml (1 tbsp) flour with each one. Add the remaining ingredients and stir in the warm fruit and juice to make a very soft dropping consistency.

4. Pour the mixture into the prepared mould and level the surface.

5. Cook, uncovered, on MEDIUM-LOW (30%) for 45-50 mins until a wooden cocktail stick, inserted in the cake, comes out clean.

6. Leave to stand for 20 mins, then turn out on to a cooling rack lined with non-stick paper. Strip off the paper and allow the cake to cool (any moisture on the surface will dry as it cools).

APPLE AND SPICE CAKE

Cooking time: about 10 mins

Serves 16

❄

450g (1 lb) eating apples, peeled, cored and finely chopped
100g (4 oz) plain white flour
100g (4 oz) plain wholemeal flour
10ml (2 tsp) baking powder
7.5ml (1½ tsp) ground mixed spice
175g (6 oz) soft brown sugar
100g (4 oz) soft margarine
2 eggs
90ml (6 tbsp) milk
sifted icing sugar, to serve

1. Grease a 1.6 litre (2¾ pt) ring mould and line the base with microwave or non-stick paper. Arrange one-third of the apple on top of the paper.

2. Put the white and wholemeal flours, baking powder, spice, sugar, margarine, eggs and milk into a large bowl and beat until smooth.

3. Fold in the remaining apple.

4. Spoon the mixture into the ring mould and level the top.

5. Cook, uncovered, for 9-10 mins or until the surface is still slightly moist but the cake beneath it is cooked.

6. Leave to stand for 15 mins, then turn the cake out on to a plate. Dust with icing sugar to serve. Delicious served warm with cream, yoghurt or crème fraîche.

VICTORIA SANDWICH CAKE

Serves 8-10

Cooking time: about 7 mins

❄

175g (6 oz) self-raising flour
175g (6 oz) soft butter or margarine
175g (6 oz) caster sugar
3 eggs
45ml (3 tbsp) milk
jam
icing sugar

1. Lightly butter a 20.5cm (8 in) soufflé dish and line its base with a circle of microwave or non-stick paper.

2. Put the flour, butter, sugar, eggs and milk in a bowl and beat until smooth. Spoon the mixture into the dish.

3. Put the dish on a microwave rack and cook, uncovered, for 6-7 mins or until risen. The surface should still be slightly moist at the centre top, but the cake beneath it should be cooked.

4. Leave to stand for 5 mins (and the surface will dry and finish cooking), then turn out on to a wire rack lined with non-stick paper. Leave to cool completely.

5. Split and fill with jam, and sieve icing sugar over the top to serve.

CARROT CAKE WITH CREAM CHEESE TOPPING

Serves 6-8

Cooking time: about 10 mins ❄

100g (4 oz) soft butter or margarine
100g (4 oz) muscovado sugar
2 eggs
grated rind and juice of a small lemon
10ml (2 tsp) ground mixed spice
15g (½ oz) desiccated coconut
100g (4 oz) carrots, finely grated
40g (1½ oz) ground almonds
100g (4 oz) self-raising flour
75g (3 oz) cream cheese
50g (2 oz) icing sugar
15ml (1 tbsp) lemon juice
25-50g (1-2 oz) walnut halves

1. Lightly butter a 1.6 litre (2¾ pt) ring mould.

2. Put the butter and brown sugar into a bowl and beat until light and fluffy. Beat in the eggs, one at a time. Add the lemon rind and juice, spice, coconut and carrots and beat well. Add the almonds, sift in the flour and fold in with a metal spoon. Spoon the mixture into the mould and level the surface.

3. Cook, uncovered, for 8-10 mins or until the cake is firm to the touch.

4. Leave to stand for 10 mins before turning out on to a wire rack lined with non-stick paper. Leave to cool completely.

5. Put the cheese, icing sugar and lemon juice in a bowl and beat until smooth. Spread it over the cake and decorate with walnuts.

ALMOND SLICES

Cooking time: about 4 mins

Makes 6
❄

100g (4 oz) soft margarine
75g (3 oz) clear honey
1 egg, beaten
75g (3 oz) plain flour, sifted
75g (3 oz) ground almonds
25g (1 oz) flaked almonds, toasted
sifted icing sugar, to serve

1. Lightly grease a 20.5cm (8 in) flan dish and line the base with microwave or non-stick paper.

2. Beat the margarine and honey until light and fluffy. Beat in the egg, then fold in the flour and ground almonds.

3. Tip the mixture into the prepared dish and level the top. Sprinkle the flaked almonds over the top. Sit the dish on a microwave rack and cook, uncovered, for about 4 mins until firm.

4. Leave to stand for 5 mins in the dish, then turn out on to a cooling rack. Leave to cool completely before cutting into wedges.

5. Dust with icing sugar to serve.

MICROWAVE MERINGUES
Makes about 24

Cooking time: about 6 mins

1 egg white
275-350g (10-12 oz) icing sugar
whipped cream and fresh fruit, to serve

1. Lightly whisk the egg white to break it up. Sift the icing sugar to remove all lumps. Line the microwave turntable, or a large heatproof plate, with microwave or non-stick paper.

2. Beat the icing sugar into the egg white, a little at a time, until you have a firm fondant-like paste.

3. Divide the mixture and shape into small balls. Arrange eight at a time, in a circle, on the paper. Cook, uncovered, for $1\frac{1}{2}$-2 mins until risen and firm to the touch (take care not to overcook them).

4. Repeat with the remaining mixture.

5. Leave to cool before carefully lifting them off the paper (they crumble easily). Serve with whipped cream and fresh fruit.

SHORTBREAD

Cooking time: about 4 mins

110g (4 oz) soft butter
50g (2 oz) caster sugar, plus extra for sprinkling
150g (5 oz) plain flour
25g (1 oz) semolina

1. Grease an 18cm (7 in) flan dish or plate and line the base with microwave or non-stick paper.

2. Beat the butter and sugar together until light and fluffy.

3. Sift the flour and semolina. Fold them into the mixture, then lightly knead it to form a dough.

4. Press the dough into the dish or plate and level the surface. Prick well with a fork. Cook for about 4 mins or until set.

5. Leave to stand for 5 mins then mark into wedges and sprinkle with extra caster sugar. Cool completely before lifting them off the paper.

CHOCOLATE BISCUIT BISCUITS   *Makes 10*
Cooking time: about 3 mins

100g (4 oz) plain chocolate
100g (4 oz) butter
15ml (1 tbsp) clear honey
30ml (2 tbsp) double cream
100g (4 oz) digestive biscuits, crumbled
50g (2 oz) chopped nuts
25g (1 oz) no-soak dried apricots, finely chopped
25g (1 oz) glacé cherries, chopped

1. Lightly grease a 20.5cm (8 in) flan dish and line the base with microwave or non-stick paper.

2. Break the chocolate into a large bowl. Cut the butter into cubes and add to the chocolate with the honey. Cook on MEDIUM (50%) for about 3 mins, stirring frequently, until melted.

3. Stir in the remaining ingredients.

4. Tip the mixture into the prepared dish and level the top. Chill until just set, mark into 10 wedges, then chill until firm.

FLAPJACKS

Cooking time: about 4-5 mins

Makes 16   ❄

75g (3 oz) butter
50g (2 oz) soft brown sugar
30ml (2 tbsp) golden syrup
175g (6 oz) porridge oats

1. Grease a shallow 12.5 x 23cm (5 x 9 in) dish.

2. Put the butter, sugar and syrup in a bowl and cook for about 2 mins, stirring once, until the sugar has dissolved. Stir well, then add the oats. Stir well again.

3. Tip the mixture into the dish and press it in well. Stand the dish on a microwave rack and cook for 2-3 mins until firm to the touch.

4. Leave to cool slightly before marking into 16 pieces. Cool completely before turning out of the dish.

WHITE CHOCOLATE CLUSTERS

Cooking time: about 8 mins   *Makes 12 sweets*

40g (1½ oz) flaked almonds
75g (3 oz) white chocolate
25g (1 oz) crystallised ginger, finely chopped
25g (1 oz) no-soak dried apricots, finely chopped

1. Put the almonds in a shallow ovenproof dish and cook for 3-4 mins, stirring frequently, until lightly browned.

2. Break the chocolate into a bowl and cook on MEDIUM-LOW (30%) for about 4 mins, stirring occasionally, until melted. Stir in the almonds, ginger and apricots.

3. Put small spoonfuls of the mixture into paper sweet cases and chill until firm.

CHOCOLATE TRUFFLES

Cooking time: about 3 mins

Makes about 24

❄

100g (4 oz) plain chocolate
50g (2 oz) butter
100g (4 oz) trifle sponges
25g (1 oz) icing sugar
15ml (1 tbsp) brandy or rum
cocoa powder, icing sugar or chocolate vermicelli

1. Break the chocolate into a bowl and add the butter. Cook on MEDIUM (50%) for 2-3 mins, stirring frequently, until melted.

2. Finely crumble the sponges and sieve the sugar. Stir the sponge crumbs, sugar and brandy or rum into the chocolate.

3. Leave to cool for about 30 mins until firm enough to handle.

4. Shape into small balls and coat them with sifted cocoa powder or icing sugar or chocolate vermicelli. Refrigerate until firm.

CORNFLAKE CRISPIES
Makes 12

Cooking time: about 5 mins

225g (8 oz) plain chocolate
50g (2 oz) butter
15ml (1 tbsp) golden syrup
50g (2 oz) cornflakes

1. Break the chocolate into a medium bowl and add the butter and syrup. Cook on MEDIUM (50%) for 4-5 mins, stirring frequently, until melted.

2. Fold in the cornflakes.

3. Put spoonfuls into paper cake cases and chill until set.

MUESLI BITES
Makes about 28

Cooking time:about 3 mins.

100g (4 oz) plain chocolate
50g (2 oz) butter
50g (2 oz) golden syrup
225g (8 oz) breakfast muesli

1. Break the chocolate into a bowl and add the butter and syrup. Cook on MEDIUM (50%) for about 3 mins, stirring frequently, until melted.

2. Stir in the muesli.

3. Put small spoonfuls of the mixture into paper sweet cases and allow to cool until set.

ALMOND AND COCONUT FUDGE

Makes 16 slices

Cooking time: about 1 min ❄

50g (2 oz) plain chocolate
50g (2 oz) unsalted butter
50g (2 oz) muscovado sugar
15ml (1 tbsp) milk
25g (1 oz) ground almonds
50g (2 oz) macaroons, crushed
25g (1 oz) desiccated coconut
icing sugar

1. Break the chocolate into a bowl and add the butter, sugar and milk. Cook for about 1 min, stirring once or twice, until melted.

2. Stir in the almonds, macaroons and coconut. Cover and refrigerate for about 30 mins or until the mixture is firm enough to handle.

3. Tip the mixture on to a sheet of non-stick or greaseproof paper and shape it into a sausage about 23cm (9 in) long. Wrap it well, twisting the ends like a Christmas cracker. Chill for 1 hour or more.

4. Remove the paper, sieve some icing sugar over the fudge and cut it into 1cm ($^1/_2$ in) slices.

15
Preserves

The microwave is superb at making small amounts of jams, jellies, marmalades and chutneys. No more huge sticky saucepans, just a large heatproof bowl which will be easy to wash up. So next time you find yourself with too much soft fruit or a glut of tomatoes, why not try your hand at preserving in your microwave?

HANDY HINTS – PRESERVES

- Use a very large bowl and make sure it will be able to withstand the high temperatures reached when boiling sugar.
- Preserves get very hot, so always use oven gloves and take care lifting the bowl out of the microwave.
- Don't try to cook more than 1.5kg (3 lb) of fruit or vegetables at one time. If you want to preserve a larger quantity, it's easier to do it on the hob.
- To make jam with a low-pectin fruit (such as strawberries), add lemon juice or bottled pectin to help it to set. Alternatively, use preserving sugar which contains natural pectin.
- Cook on HIGH (100%) unless the preserve threatens to boil over, in which case, lower the power to MEDIUM (50%) and cook for longer.
- Adding a knob of butter to jams and marmalades helps to reduce foaming.
- Always cook preserves uncovered. Unless the recipe states otherwise, you will need to boil it rapidly in order to drive off the steam to thicken the chutney or to set the jam.
- Check the setting points of jams, jellies and marmalades by dropping a small spoonful on to a chilled saucer – if a skin forms, it is ready to set. If not, continue cooking

for a little longer. On a microwave sugar thermometer, setting point is 220-222°F (104-105°C). Don't use a conventional sugar thermometer.

● Chutneys should be cooked until the mixture is thick and there is no pool of liquid on the surface.

● Pot all the preserves into sterilised jars (see below).

TO STERILISE JARS IN THE MICROWAVE

Quarter-fill up to four jars with water and arrange in a circle in the microwave. Bring to the boil on HIGH (100%). Using oven gloves, carefully lift the jars out of the microwave and empty out the water. Invert the jars on to a clean tea towel or kitchen paper and use as required.

JAM – Basic method

up to 1.5kg prepared fruit
equal weight of sugar
lemon juice or pectin: 30ml (2 tbsp) per 450g (1 lb)
    fruit, if required (see hints above)
knob of butter

1. Put the fruit into a large heatproof bowl with water, if necessary. Most soft fruits need no additional liquid. Fruits with skins (such as plums, gooseberries and blackcurrants) may need about 15ml (1 tbsp) per 450g (1 lb).

2. Cook until just soft, stirring occasionally. Do not overcook – to prevent spoiling the colour and flavour. Cover fruits with skins during cooking to help tenderise them.

3. Warm the sugar for 3-4 mins, either in its opened bag or in a bowl, to help it dissolve easily.

4. Add the warm sugar to the hot fruit and stir well. The sugar must dissolve before the jam boils.

5. Stir in lemon juice or pectin, if needed.

6. Cook for 12-15 mins or until setting point is reached (see page 240).

7. Stir in the butter then, using a slotted spoon, lift off any scum.

8. Allow jam with whole fruit to cool slightly before potting, to prevent the fruit rising to the top of the jars. Otherwise, pour immediately, filling hot sterilised jars to 0.5cm ($\frac{1}{4}$ in) from the top.

9. Put a waxed paper circle on the surface of the jam, cover, and label it.

JELLIES – Basic method

up to 1.5kg prepared fruit
equal weight of sugar
lemon juice or pectin: 30ml (2 tbsp) per 450g (1 lb)
fruit if required - (see page 239)

1. Cook the fruit as in stage 1 for Jam (page 240).

2. Strain the mixture through a jelly bag or muslin to extract the juice. Leave it to strain until the juice has stopped dripping through - don't be tempted to squeeze the bag or the jelly will cloud.

3. Measure the juice. Weigh 450g (1 lb) sugar for each 600ml (1 pt) juice.

4. Heat the juice in a large heatproof bowl for about 5 mins until warm.

5. Warm the sugar as in stage 4 for Jam (page 240).

6. Continue with stages 5-9 for Jam.

MARMALADE - Basic method
Makes about 1kg (2½ lb)

2 lemons
1kg (2 lb) Seville oranges
1kg (2 lb) sugar
knob of butter

1. Warm the lemons for 1 min. Squeeze their juice into a large bowl.

2. Cut the rind from the oranges, avoiding the white pith. Cut the rind into shred and set aside.

3. Put the orange flesh and pips into a food processor and chop. Add the mixture to the lemon juice with 900ml (1½ pt) boiling water. Cover and cook for about 15 mins.

4. Tip the mixture into a sieve over a large heatproof bowl, pressing until all the juice is extracted. Stir the orange rind into the juice and cook for about 15 mins, stirring occasionally, until the rind is tender.

5. Add the sugar, stirring to dissolve it completely. Cook, uncovered, for about 10 mins, stirring once, until setting point is reached (see page 240).

6. Stir in the butter then, using a slotted spoon, remove any scum.

7. Leave to cool for 15 mins then pot, cover and label.

RASPBERRY JAM

Makes about 700g (1¹/₂ lb)

450g (1 lb) raspberries
450g (1 lb) caster sugar

1. Put the raspberries into a large heatproof bowl and cook for about 4 mins or until the fruit is soft, stirring once or twice.
2. Add the sugar and stir well. Cook for 2 mins, stirring frequently, until the sugar has dissolved.
3. Cook, uncovered, for about 10-12 mins, stirring occasionally, until setting point is reached (see page 240).
4. Cool slightly and pour into hot sterilised jars, cover and label.

LEMON CURD

Makes about 900kg (2 lb)

grated rind and juice of 4 lemons
100g (4 oz) unsalted butter, diced
450g (1 lb) caster sugar
four size 2 eggs, beaten

1. Put the lemon rind and juice into a large heatproof bowl. Add the butter and sugar. Cook for about 4 mins until the butter has melted. Stir well.
2. Mix the eggs into the lemon mixture.
3. Cook, uncovered, for 5-6 mins, stirring or whisking well every minute, until the mixture is thick and creamy.
4. Whisk for 1 minute then leave to cool slightly and pour into hot sterilised jars, cover and label.
5. Store in the refrigerator for up to 2-3 weeks.

MINT JELLY

Makes about 900g (2 lb)

40g (1¹/₂ oz) fresh mint leaves
450g (1 lb) caster sugar
300ml (¹/₂ pt) white wine vinegar
225ml (8 fl oz) bottled pectin (Certo)
green food colouring
15g (¹/₂ oz) finely chopped fresh mint

1. Put the mint leaves, sugar and vinegar in a large heatproof bowl. Cook for 8-10 mins or until the sugar dissolves, stirring occasionally.

2. Cook for 1-2 mins or until the mixture boils.

3. Strain the mixture through a fine nylon sieve, muslin or a jelly bag (do not be tempted to squeeze it through, or the jelly will cloud).

4. Stir the pectin into the juice and add a little food colouring.

5. Cook, uncovered, for 4-5 mins, stirring occasionally.

6. Stir in the chopped mint. Leave to cool slightly, then pour into hot sterilised jars, cover and label.

APPLE BUTTER

Makes about 2kg (4 lb)

up to 1kg (2 lb) cooking apples or sharp eating apples
sugar
butter
5ml (1 tsp) ground cinnamon

1. Cook the fruit as in stage 1 for Jam (page 240). Don't bother to peel or core the apples - just chop them.

2. Push the mixture through a nylon sieve and weigh the purée.

3. Weigh out 350g (12 oz) sugar and 25g (1 oz) butter for each 450g (1 lb) fruit purée.

4. Warm the sugar as in stage 4 for Jam (page 240).

5. Put the fruit purée into a large heatproof bowl and stir in the warm sugar, butter and cinnamon.

   Continue as for stages 5-9 for Jam (page 241).

BEETROOT AND APPLE CHUTNEY

Makes about 1.5kg (3 lb)

450g (1 lb) small whole beetroot, scrubbed
450g (1 lb) cooking apples, peeled, cored and diced
225g (8 oz) onions, finely chopped
450ml (³/₄ pt) red or white wine vinegar
2.5ml (¹/₂ tsp) ground cumin
2.5ml (¹/₂ tsp) celery salt
2.5ml (¹/₂ tsp) salt

1. Put the beetroot into a large bowl with 60ml (4 tbsp) water. Cover and cook for 7-8 mins or until tender. Drain and leave to cool, then remove the skin and finely chop the beetroot.

2. Put the apples into a large heatproof bowl and add the onion, vinegar, spice and salt. Cover and cook for about 5 mins until the onion is soft, stirring once.

3. Stir in the beetroot, cover and cook for 10 mins.

4. Uncover and cook, stirring occasionally (and frequently when the mixture thickens), until the chutney is thick and there is no pool of liquid.

5. Leave to cool slightly, then spoon into hot sterilised jars, cover and label.

TOMATO CHUTNEY

Makes about 900g (2 lb)

700g (1½ lb) firm tomatoes
225g (8 oz) cooking apples, peeled, cored and chopped
1 medium onion, finely chopped
100g (4 oz) muscovado sugar
100g (4 oz) sultanas
5ml (1 tsp) salt
200ml (7 fl oz) malt vinegar
15g (½ oz) ground ginger
2.5ml (½ tsp) mustard powder
1.25ml (¼ tsp) cayenne pepper

1. Put the tomatoes into a large heatproof bowl and pour over sufficient boiling water to just cover them. Cook for about 4 mins then, one at a time, lift the tomatoes out of the water and remove and discard their skins. Roughly chop the tomatoes.

2. Put all the ingredients into a large heatproof bowl and mix well. Cook, uncovered, for about 30 mins, stirring occasionally (and frequently when the mixture thickens), or until the chutney is thick and there is no pool of liquid.

3. Leave to cool slightly then spoon into hot sterilised jars, cover and label.

16

All the Extras

SOFTEN BUTTER
Heat on MEDIUM-LOW (30%). 100g (4 oz) takes about 30 secs.

MELT CHOCOLATE
Break the chocolate into a bowl and heat on MEDIUM (50%), stirring frequently, until just melted. Take care not to overheat it.

DRINKS
Reheat fresh coffee, make instant coffee and tea, or heat milk and fruit drinks in the microwave. You get best results by:
● using a large cup or mug, with sloping sides (where the top is slightly wider than the bottom). Don't try and heat milk in a milk bottle.

● stirring the drink before putting it into the microwave and occasionally during heating.

● heating on HIGH (100%) – 1 cup or mug takes about 1½-2 mins. Should the drink threaten to boil over, use a lower power level.

DISSOLVE GELATINE
1. Measure 45ml (3 tbsp) water, or liquid from your recipe, into a small bowl. Sprinkle over an 11g packet gelatine. Leave it to stand for a few mins until the granules have absorbed the liquid and look like a 'sponge'.

2. Stir it into a hot mixture (such as custard) until it has dissolved. Alternatively, heat the 'sponge' on MEDIUM (50%) for about 1 min, stirring frequently, until all the granules have dissolved (*do not allow gelatine to boil*

or it won't set) then leave it to cool slightly before quickly stirring it in a cold mixture.

JELLY
1. Break up a fruit jelly tablet into a measuring jug which will hold at least 600ml (1 pt). Add sufficient cold water just to cover it.

2. Heat for about 2 mins or until the jelly has just dissolved. Stir well.

3. Add sufficient cold water or fruit juice to make the jelly up to 600ml (1 pt).

4. Pour into a dish and chill until set.

SOFTEN JAM, JELLY, SYRUP OR HONEY
Soften jam for filling cakes or heat syrup or honey for easy pouring. Heat, uncovered, on MEDIUM (50%), stirring frequently. Syrup and honey can be softened in their jars (but not in cans). Take care – these high-sugar foods will become very hot very quickly.

CROUTONS
1. Thinly spread two slices of bread on both sides with plain or garlic butter. Trim off and discard the crusts. Cut the bread into 1cm ($^1/_2$ in) cubes.

2. Spread the cubes in an even layer on a plate and cook, uncovered, for about 3 mins, stirring once or twice. The croûtons will continue to crispen on cooling. These are best used on the day they are made.

CRISPY BREADCRUMBS
Use these as a topping to add colour and crunch to microwaved food, or as a delicious addition to fresh salads.

1. Put 50g (2 oz) butter in a bowl and heat for about $1^1/_2$ mins until melted.

2. Stir in 100g (4 oz) fresh breadcrumbs, mixing them well. Spread the mixture in a shallow dish or on a heatproof plate.

3. Cook, uncovered, for about 4-5 mins, stirring frequently, until crisp and light golden brown.

4. Leave to cool completely and store in an airtight jar.

MELBA TOAST
1. Toast a slice of bread on both sides (in a toaster or under a grill).

2. Trim and discard the crusts then slice the bread in half horizontally (between the toasted sides) to make two thin slices. Cut each slice in half.

3. Arrange, untoasted side up, on a large plate or on the turntable. Cook for about 40 secs until dry, crisp and curled.

TOAST NUTS
1. Spread 100g (4 oz) flaked or chopped nuts in an even layer in a shallow dish.

2. Cook, uncovered, for about 4-5 mins, stirring frequently, or until golden brown.

3. Leave to cool completely and store in an airtight jar.

TOAST COCONUT
1. Spread some desiccated coconut in an even layer in a shallow dish.

2. Cook, stirring frequently, until it has turned a light golden brown. Take care not to overheat it – coconut easily burns.

ORANGES AND LEMONS
You will be able to squeeze extra juice from oranges and lemons by warming them in the microwave first. Heat them for 1-2 mins.

SOFTEN SUGAR
Sugar that has become hard can be softened in its packet. Heat it for 30-40 secs.

SOFTEN MARZIPAN
Remove any foil packaging. Put the marzipan on a sheet of kitchen paper and cook for 1-2 mins or until soft and easy to work.

SOFTEN ICE CREAM
Soften solid ice cream but take care not to overheat and melt it. Heat on LOW (10%) until soft enough to spoon out of the tub. 1 litre ($1^3/_4$ pt) will take about 2 mins.

POPPADUMS
With oil:
Brush one side of a poppadum with a little oil and put it on a sheet of paper towel. Cook for about 1 min until crisp and puffed up.

Without oil:
Put two poppadums on a sheet of paper towel and cook for 1-$1^1/_2$ mins or until crisp and puffed up.

DRY HERBS
1. Arrange the leaves of fresh herbs in a single layer on a sheet of kitchen paper.
2. Cook, turning or stirring them every 30 secs, until they are dry and will crumble between your fingers.
3. Leave to cool completely and store in an airtight jar.

WARM PLATES
This is only worth doing if you have no other means of warming plates. Put a little water between the plates and on the top one. Heat for $1/_2$-1 min until warm. Drain, dry and use them immediately.

Index

Recipes which Serve One or Two